above all

A

take up & READ

PUBLICATION

Managing Editor: Elizabeth Foss

Research & Development: Elizabeth Foss, Emily DeArdo

Copy Editors: Emily DeArdo, Rosie Hill, Allison McGinley

Cover Art and Illustration by: Christie Peters

Calligraphy by: Rakhi McCormick

Design and Illustration by: Kristin Foss

Copyright © 2017 Take Up and Read

ISBN-13: 978-1983754531
ISBN-10: 1983754536

COMMUNITY

VISIT US

takeupandread.org

BE SOCIAL

Facebook @takeupandread

Instagram @takeupandread

Twitter @totakeupandread

SEND A NOTE

totakeupandread@gmail.com

CONNECT

#TakeUpAndRead

#AboveAll

HOW?

HOW WILL THE TIRED SOUL
LIVING IN THE WOMAN
IN THE MIDDLE OF WINTER GRAY
BE ENERGIZED BY THE BEGINNING
OF A SEASON OF PENANCE?

HOW WILL SHE FIND HOPE
AND NEW ENERGY IN THE
HARD WORK OF REPENTING?

SHE WILL PRAY—MORE.

BEFORE YOU BEGIN: LECTIO DIVINA

Together, as a community of faithful women, today at the beginning of Lent, we are ready for a spiritual springtime. We are ready for new life— for a spiritual renewal of our minds, hearts, and souls. We are embracing Lent as a season to change our hearts and prepare the soil of our souls for the risen Christ.

How? How will the tired soul living in the woman in the middle of winter gray be energized by the beginning of a season of penance? How will she find hope and new energy in the hard work of repenting?

She will pray—more. That's right. She will take more time to pray even though so many things pull on her time. Can we do that together? Can we take up for ourselves the ancient tradition of *lectio divina* and let the Word lead us to live in charity? We can and we must. This is the best way to prepare ourselves for the miracle of the Resurrection with peaceful composure and serene grace.

In his 2010 apostolic exhortation *Verbum Domini*, Pope Benedict XVI beautifully instructs the faithful to prayerfully read the Scripture. Following his lead, we will be drawn into a practice that is as old as Scripture itself. We will closely read and ponder Scripture passages carefully chosen for this season.

In the early Christian communities, Scripture was read to nourish faith with the wisdom of truth. When we hold the New Testament, we take up the understanding that the first Christians had of the Old Testament, together with the divine revelation the Holy Spirit granted to Jesus' earliest followers.

The Church Fathers' faith was informed by their careful, prayerful reading of the Word. Today, we are blessed to welcome their wisdom into our reading when we access the commentaries that were the fruit of their lectio. The monastic movement grew in the fertile soil of lectio divina. The daily, ordered life of the monks was (and is) centered upon spiritual reading of Scripture. Can ordinary women in the twenty-first century find spiritual nourishment and new life in this age-old practice of holy men?

We can.

There are five steps in the pattern, five distinct movements that will direct the way we travel through our days. First, we read. Then, a meditation engages the mind, using reason to search for knowledge in the message. The prayer is the movement of the heart towards God, a beseeching on behalf of the soul. The contemplation elevates the mind and suspends it in God's presence. Finally, the action is the way we live our lives as gift of charity towards others. It's a tall order, but it's the very best way to live.

Let's take a careful look at each step.

Pope Benedict writes, "It opens with the reading (lectio) of a text, which leads to a desire to understand its true content: what does the biblical text say in itself." (Verbum Domini, 87). This is where we explore the literary genre of the text, the characters we meet in the story, and the objective meaning intended by the author. We usually offer several passages which work together towards a common theme; you can choose just one passage, or you can look at the group together, as the Holy Spirit inspires. A good study Bible and/or a Bible dictionary will help you to place the reading in context.

"Next comes meditation (meditatio), which asks: what does the biblical text say to us?" (DV, 87) Prayerfully we ponder what personal message the text holds for each of us and what effect that message should have on our lives.

"Following this comes prayer (oratio), which asks the question: what do we say to the Lord in response to his word? Prayer, as petition, intercession, thanksgiving and praise, is the primary way by which the word transforms us." (DV, 87) What do we say to God in response to His Word? We ask Him what He desires of us. We ask Him for the strength and grace to do His will. Moved by His mercy, we give him thanks and praise.

The fourth act is "contemplation (contemplatio), during which we take up, as a gift from God, His own way of seeing and judging reality, and ask ourselves what conversion of mind, heart and life is the Lord asking of us?" (DV, 87) Here, reflect on how God has conveyed His love for us in the day's Scripture. Recognize the beauty of His gifts and the goodness of His mercy and rest in that. Let God light you from within and look out on the world in a new way because you have been transformed by the process of prayerful Scripture study.

Finally, the whole point of this time we've taken from our day is to get up from the reading and go live the Gospel. Actio is where we make an act of our wills and resolve to bring the text to life in our lives. This is our fiat. "The process of lectio divina is not concluded until it arrives at action (actio), which moves the believer to make his or her life a gift for others in charity. We find the supreme synthesis and fulfillment of this process in the Mother of God. For every member of the faithful Mary is the model of docile acceptance of God's word, for she 'kept all these things, pondering them in her heart.'" (Lk 2:19; cf. 2:51) (DV, 87)

Together, this Lent, we will endeavor to engage in lectio divina every day. To correlate with each day's Scripture passages, we've created pages for your time of prayer, and we've created pages for your active time. We want this book to come alive in your hands, to bring you a spiritual springtime. Try to take the time each day to dig deep, but if you have to cut your time short, don't be discouraged. Ask the Blessed Mother to help you find pockets throughout the day to re-engage. You don't have to fill in every box. There is no right or wrong answer. And you don't have to dig deeply with every passage.

Pray the parts you can, and trust the Holy Spirit to water it well in your soul. Know that God can do loaves and fishes miracles with your small parcels of time, if only you are willing to offer Him what you have. Before Lent gets swallowed with the ordinary to-do lists of seasonal hustle, sit in prayer and see how you can tune your heart to the beat of the Lord's, and ensure that the best gift you give this season is your life, given for others in charity.

FINALLY, THE ACTION IS THE WAY WE LIVE OUR LIVES AS GIFT OF CHARITY TOWARDS OTHERS. IT'S A TALL ORDER, BUT IT'S THE VERY BEST WAY TO LIVE.

LECTIO

2 Timothy 3:16-17
Written by St. Paul from prison to St. Timothy, who was in Ephesus.
"All scripture" means all of the Old Testament but also maybe some
of the Gospel accounts that became part of the New Testament.

MEDITATIO

What personal message
does the text have for me?

The social media feeds I choose can compete with the message of the gospel. Scripture can be trusted. It should be my go-to when preparing for everything. my inspiration more than the internet.

ORATIO

What do I say to the Lord in
response to His word?

Thank you for giving for giving me your Word. Remind me through out my day, when I lose my way and look to other sources of direction, that You have everything I need to do Your good work.

CONTEMPLATIO

What conversion of mind,
heart, and life is He asking
of me today?

I think God is reminding me to get the ratio right: consult Scripture more than other things that compete for my time and attention.

How did I progress in living the Word today?

INTENTIONAL DESIGN

Each of our studies is created with unique, intentional design. We want to connect you with the Word and keep you connected throughout the season of Lent. In this Scripture study, we provided scholarly research to guide you through the ancient practice of lectio divina ("holy reading") . We added new design layouts, font design, and original artwork to ensure you have the tools to keep Him close to your heart, every day.

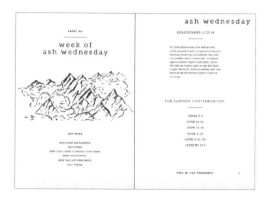

In this book, we will work on memorizing Colossians 3:12-17 throughout the season of Lent.

DAILY SCRIPTURE READING
This Scripture study includes daily Scripture readings, with margins for your notes. Notations for further reading are provided so you can open your Bible and further explore the Word.

LECTIO DIVINA
Reflect upon the Word and make a deep connection with your daily life.

ACTIO
Throughout Lent, the Actio will change with intention to prepare your heart for Easter.

PRAY
Start a conversation with God on the page and continue it in your heart.

At Take Up & Read, we want you to discover what prompts and pages are most useful to you. There is no perfect way to perform lectio—the important thing is that you take the time to have a conversation with God, using His Word as your guide.

A NOTE FROM THE COVER ARTIST

In fall 2017, I watched as my beloved hometown of Houston was taken underwater by Hurricane Harvey. I posted a painting I'd done of the San Fernando Cathedral in San Antonio, Texas, on my social media and reflected on the resilience of human nature and the way our community was slowly knitting itself back together. I will never forget those days. Most importantly, the beauty of humans helping humans was above all else. The painting I shared that day is the one on our cover.

One of my favorite things is taking my watercolor set on plane rides. I sit there the whole time, nose pressed against the window, trying to absorb every little visual detail while the earth is far below. I can't tell you how many times I've sat there in my tiny plane chair and painted the mountain ranges below me. The drawings inside these pages are pieced together from my sketchbooks, little snippets of time where everything else has just faded away and my world came into focus through paint and paper.

Mountains are forever steady yet equally dynamic. They are firmly planted but constantly change as the light hits them and the world keeps turning. When I heard the title and concept of the Lenten journal this year, I was immediately captivated by how a life with Christ is truly "above all." It is our highest calling. It means we rise above this contentious cultural climate, and it is the most important part of our lives we can develop. I pray that these illustrations offer you the peace of Christ as you meditate with this beautiful and thoughtful journal.

CHRISTIE PETERS

above all

A

take up & READ

PUBLICATION

GENESIS 3:1-9

Now the serpent was more subtle than any other wild creature that the Lord God had made. He said to the woman, "Did God say, 'You shall not eat of any tree of the garden'?" And the woman said to the serpent, "We may eat of the fruit of the trees of the garden; but God said, 'You shall not eat of the fruit of the tree which is in the midst of the garden, neither shall you touch it, lest you die.'" But the serpent said to the woman, "You will not die. For God knows that when you eat of it your eyes will be opened, and you will be like God, knowing good and evil." So when the woman saw that the tree was good for food, and that it was a delight to the eyes, and that the tree was to be desired to make one wise, she took of its fruit and ate; and she also gave some to her husband, and he ate. Then the eyes of both were opened, and they knew that they were naked; and they sewed fig leaves together and made themselves aprons. And they heard the sound of the Lord God walking in the garden in the cool of the day, and the man and his wife hid themselves from the presence of the Lord God among the trees of the garden. But the Lord God called to the man, and said to him, "Where are you?"

**BUT THE LORD GOD
CALLED TO THE MAN,
AND SAID TO HIM,
"WHERE ARE YOU?"**

GENESIS 3:9

INTRODUCTION

Welcome.

My little girls all say it was about an apple. My little boys always said it was Eve's fault. In truth, it was about wanting to be God—as knowledgeable, as powerful, as formidable as God. From the very beginning, all good things which come from God, every piece of perfect that Eden provided, has been bulldozed by creatures. He is good and He gives us the will to do what we choose. Since that day with the apple, we tend to choose poorly, often because we want to be God rather than being like God, and evil wrestles with good, making for real human suffering. We are prideful, imperfect people who need a real way to stop rebelling against our good God much more than we need Lent to be a six-week self-improvement plan.

Since the day with the apple, sin has been lying to us. It has promised us things it can't deliver and deceived us with the notion that God has held back, that somehow He neglected to give us the very best He had. The serpent sowed seeds of doubt in a garden of perfect joy by whispering the lie that God's motives weren't all good.

All the gorgeous glory of the garden was shrouded in a cloud of shame when Adam and Eve committed that very first sin. Pride gave birth to shame. Pride told them that they had to strive to attain the best things all on their own, apart from God. Pride lied and said they wouldn't die. But they did. And so will we.

And, frankly, we all deserve to die because over and over again we think we need something that is outside God's provision and we scamper off after it, only to find ourselves digging our graves along a path to nowhere. We are offered glory and we choose destruction.

Over and over again.

It's crazy. We choose the happy of the moment over the joy of the eternal. It's truly sick. And only God can heal.

Adam and Eve committed a sin that condemned the entire human race. Now, we commit our own sins. We all sin and fall short of the glory of God. (Romans 3:23) Our hope is not in curing ourselves. We just can't.

Our hope is in knowing the good God who created us. Our hope is in drawing so close to Him that, instead of wanting to be Him, we want to be like Him, and we want what He wants for us. Our hope is in returning to Him with our whole hearts. Our hope is in holding nothing back, returning to Eden, naked and vulnerable before an all-loving God. We want true authenticity. We want to be the genuine images of Himself that He created us to be.

Draw close to the One who heals. He has a promise for you, and for me, this Lent. Ask Him to show you your sin. Ask Him for both the strength and the humility to repent. Ask Him to heal your heart.

He is calling you into His abundant grace. Go.

If, because of the one man's trespass, death exercised dominion through that one, much more surely will those who receive the abundance of grace and the free gift of righteousness exercise dominion in life through the one man, Jesus Christ.

ROMANS 5:17

ELIZABETH FOSS

OUR HOPE IS IN HOLDING NOTHING BACK, RETURNING TO EDEN, NAKED AND VULNERABLE BEFORE AN ALL-LOVING GOD. WE WANT TRUE AUTHENTICITY. WE WANT TO BE THE GENUINE IMAGES OF HIMSELF THAT HE CREATED US TO BE.

week of
ash wednesday

EVERY DAY THIS WEEK:

SCRIPTURE READINGS

ESSAY REFLECTION

LECTIO DIVINA

ACTIO REFLECTION

PRAYER

ash wednesday

COLOSSIANS 3:12-14

As God's chosen ones, holy and beloved,
clothe yourselves with compassion, kindness,
humility, meekness, and patience. Bear with
one another and, if anyone has a complaint
against another, forgive each other; just as
the Lord has forgiven you, so you also must
forgive. Above all, clothe yourselves with love,
which binds everything together in perfect
harmony.

FOR FURTHER CONTEMPLATION:

JAMES 4:6

JOHN 14:26

JOHN 16:13

MARK 6:31

JOHN 8:31-32

HEBREWS 11:1

Faith is the realization of what is hoped for and evidence of things not seen. Hebrews 11:1

The humble soul listens well. For the next few days, we are going to take a good look at listening in order to understand how pride makes bad listeners of us and how good, humble listening opens the floodgates of grace. It's important to cultivate the ability to listen well, both to God and to the people God has put in our lives. If we are poor listeners to the human voices around us, chances are good that something even more troubling is happening. Chances are we are poor listeners to the Holy Spirit. Listening well is a habit; the people we know help us cultivate that habit.

If we can't listen to our children, or our spouses, or our friends, we probably aren't listening to God either; we're babbling on and on in His presence, failing to let Him get a word in edgewise. The relationship is dying. You're having a one-way conversation with the Lord of the Universe. That seems a waste.

Or, even worse, we're not encountering Him in conversation at all.

Before closely examining how to listen well to human voices, let's spend some time evaluating how well we listen to the Holy Spirit.

Are we able to be quiet and gentle? God wants us to come away with Him to a quiet place—to stop talking, to still the anxious thoughts that crowd our heads and keep us away from His peace. Those distractions that tell you that you don't have time to sit in stillness with the Holy Spirit are actually tools of the devil. If we're honest, we all have time, because all time really belongs to God. If He matters to you, listen to Him.

Offer to God the same thoughtfulness and respect that you would offer to a client or to the doctor. Prepare for your time in His presence. Reflect on the pieces of your life: your words, your actions, your plans, your fears, your failures. Bring them to Him, but don't babble on. Just lay them at the foot of the cross, stand back a bit, and be still in His presence.

God offers freedom to the children who love Him. He doesn't hold himself back, but He does ask us to meet Him and to hear Him. He speaks to us in His word. The more we stop and steep ourselves in His word, the more intimate we become with His Spirit. We begin to understand the way He works and to anticipate His responses as we go about our lives. His voice is the one we hear in our heads. This familiarity, this easy, comfortable way of being together, is the intimate conversation between lovers. This is love.

The Holy Spirit is pursuing you. He wants this kind of love with you.

As our conversations grow more familiar, our faith blossoms into one of confident assurance. We know He's there and He's ours. It becomes an eternal love affair where trust drives the relationship. That trust gives us the courage to know that the Holy Spirit will lead us to the right path and equip us with everything we need to walk it well. Faith grown in a relationship with the Holy Spirit emboldens us and matures us spiritually.

He comes to us in Holy Communion, physically present, and we bring Him into ourselves, to the very depths of our being. It is sacramental intimacy. But He wants to be heard, too. His voice is quiet and gentle. He wants the sweet communion of conversation. Don't profane the Real Presence by denying the communication of the Spirit.

Listening to the Lord is how we put on love, how we clothe ourselves in Christ. Every day (or almost every day), you take the time to get dressed. You put on the garments of the material world. Can you find the time to put on love as well? Can you clothe yourself in God's Word and allow yourself to hear His Spirit all day?

ELIZABETH FOSS

THE HOLY SPIRIT IS PURSUING YOU.

LECTIO DIVINA

LECTIO

Colossians 3:12-14

Paul is writing to the Colossians during his first imprisonment in Rome (between 60 and 62 A.D.). He writes to address certain heresies that have sprung up among the people in Colossae, a city in Asia Minor (located in modern-day Turkey).

MEDITATIO

What personal message does the text have for me?

ORATIO

What do I say to the Lord in response to His word?

CONTEMPLATIO

What conversion of mind, heart, and life is He asking of me today?

How did I progress in living the Word today?

Ash Wednesday
REFLECTION

What is keeping you from God's Word?
How can you increase your knowledge and
understanding of the good Lord, who wants so
much to tuck Himself into your heart so that
you know His voice all day long?

PRAY

Jesus, I want to know Your voice.
Please instill in me a desire for Your Word.
Make me want to spend time with You.

thursday

JOHN 8:47

Whoever is from God hears the words of God. The reason you do not hear them is that you are not from God.

FOR FURTHER CONTEMPLATION:

SIRACH 6:33-35

SIRACH 3:17

GALATIANS 4:6-9

His blue eyes always twinkled when he spoke. And his embraces were always tight, as if he was hugging you for the last time.

He knew so much about living. When you're part of the Greatest Generation, you tend to live up to your name. That wildflower? The reason that fencepost is built a certain way? The way the clouds roll and the impending weather they foretell? When to plant tomatoes? How to maneuver the scroll saw with expertise? How to get on with the business of living, instead of dying? That, he knew better than most.

I'm speaking about my 91-year-old grandfather. As a tail gunner in World War II, he lived more at age 18 in his 37 missions than I may ever live as a mom of six kids. There were times I'd sit on the couch with him, and I would listen as he told fascinating story after fascinating story, all while showing me card tricks and spinning his yo-yo like a boss. As the years passed, the yo-yo gave way to his smartphone, and he'd show me the latest photo he'd taken or news article he'd read.

Last year, when the call came in on Holy Thursday that he had passed away, it completely broke me open. I had to pull my van over, slump over my steering wheel, and sob until the tears began to slow.

His funeral was the Monday after Easter. Lent and Holy Week took on an entirely new meaning.

Sometimes, our Lent chooses us, doesn't it?

You see, Papa was my biggest advocate, encouraging me to follow my passions: write more, spend less time worrying and more time loving. At 91, he was acutely aware of his numbered days. While the rest of the world often gave me advice, it was his I listened to. His I craved. His I curled up on the couch soak up eagerly.

These 40 days, Jesus is begging us to sit at His feet to ponder, to pray, and to take the time to develop a relationship with Him. With each sacred word of Scripture, He's embracing us tight, weaving our souls to the power of His word. He's branding us with His grace and mercy, gently guiding us into a relationship.

He, too, has a twinkle in His eyes. He made the wildflowers. He created the countrysides for us to fence in. He delights in the changing weather. He rejoices at a well-earned crop of vegetables. As a carpenter, His hands have carved the finest things; namely, us. This Lent, He wants you to get on with the business of living, instead of dying. He thirsts for your soul.

As a former Protestant and convert to Catholicism, I brought with me a great love of Scripture. God's word has been the balm to my aching, suffering, repentant heart. This Lent, if you're seeking encouragement, healing, or something in between, curl up on the couch with eager ears and your Bible in hand. Sirach says it well: "Be ready to listen to every godly discourse, and let no wise proverbs escape you." (Sirach 6:35)

My grandfather and his wise words continue to reverberate within my heart each day. Hold on tight to God, y'all. He has so much to share with you.

KATHRYN WHITAKER

BE READY TO LISTEN
TO EVERY GODLY DISCOURSE,
AND LET NO WISE
PROVERBS ESCAPE YOU.

SIRACH 6:35

LECTIO DIVINA

John 8:47
John's Gospel was probably written before 100 A.D, with the intent of convincing people that Jesus is the Christ, the Son of God (John 20:31). Earlier in this chapter, Jesus has been speaking to the people about truth and His divine origins, but the people cannot accept that He is God.

MEDITATIO

What personal message does the text have for me?

ORATIO

What do I say to the Lord in response to His word?

CONTEMPLATIO

What conversion of mind, heart, and life is He asking of me today?

How did I progress in living the Word today?

Thursday after Ash Wednesday
REFLECTION

Make a plan. Make a promise. When will you be still in conversation with the Word? This is the time that gets ink on your calendar every day. Tell Him when you'll meet Him and ask Him to help you keep the appointment. Maybe it's during carline or in the stillness of the morning. Perhaps it's during a study break, after kids' bathtimes, or in the 5.7 minutes you have to inhale lunch. Wherever you might be, look forward to that conversation with your Beloved.

PRAY

I will be here, Lord,
waiting to read your word and
hear what you have to say.
I will not be anxious about my day,
nor will I do all the talking.
I will be content to be,
to find comfort in the silence,
and hear your voice.
It's your grace and
mercy I seek Lord—
let me discover it
through your Word.

friday

1 CORINTHIANS 13: 1-2, 4, 11

If I speak in the tongues of mortals and of
angels, but do not have love, I am a noisy
gong or a clanging cymbal. And if I have
prophetic powers, and understand all
mysteries and all knowledge, and if I have all
faith, so as to remove mountains, but do not
have love, I am nothing.

...

Love is patient; love is kind; love is not
envious or boastful or arrogant or rude. ...
When I was a child, I spoke like a child, I
thought like a child, I reasoned like a child;
when I became an adult, I put an end to
childish ways.

FOR FURTHER CONTEMPLATION:

SIRACH 11:7-9
SIRACH 5:11-13
ROMANS 12:10
PROVERBS 20:5
PROVERBS 18:13

Are you a patient listener? A fool rushes into conversations and sprays herself over the scene, leaving a fine mist (or heavy coating) of her pride over everything, then coming away knowing nothing more about the people in her midst than she did when the conversation began. Good listening requires patience and humility. When we half listen and then jump right in, we presume to know more about what someone else is saying than he does. We busy ourselves in our heads with whatever response we're going to offer or we divert attention to something else entirely (iPhone much?). Our pride runs roughshod over true communication. When I only half listen—because I think I know better or more, or because I'm preoccupied with myself—I devalue the person who talks. When I listen with my full attention and fix my eyes on his face, searching for meaning, I assure him beyond a doubt that he matters. Listening requires concentration and it requires patience. We can't just hear somebody as he begins to speak and then push the conversation to the periphery of our consciousness. We need to implore the Holy Spirit for both the patience and humility to keep listening.

Listening well is an act of respect, of honor, and of selfless love. Poor listening turns a friend away, rejecting her heart. Good listening gathers her in and holds her close. This first Friday in Lent, let's give up interrupting, give up formulating answers before hearing the whole story, give up thinking we know everything.

Instead, draw deep into the well of someone's heart and be a woman of understanding. We listen with humility when we ask considerate questions. Holy meekness allows us to draw another person out and to help him understand himself better, not to know our opinions. Empathetic listening serves other people.

Truly offering full time and attention is a generous, gracious gift of self. Some of the most precious moments in my lifetime are the moments I can sit at my kitchen counter, offer a cup of something warm, look someone in the eyes, lean into his pain, and hear his heart until there is nothing left for him to say.

Good listening gives a person a hallowed place to give voice to the ponderings of soul. I think God knew that my pride would get in the way of listening well, that I so love words that the temptation is strong to let them rush in and take over. I was born with only one ear. I struggle to hear and the struggle helps me to listen. I am forced to tilt my good ear towards someone when they talk and I look intently at what they are saying in order to let those cues of eyes and lips fill in where maybe I just can't hear.

What a blessing this "curse" has been to me, because in the seeing of what someone is saying, in the necessity of paying close attention, I am granted the full vision of a heart's whole story instead of a mere glimpse into a brief message.

ELIZABETH FOSS

**GOOD LISTENING
GIVES A PERSON
A *HALLOWED PLACE*
TO GIVE VOICE
TO THE PONDERINGS
OF *SOUL*.**

LECTIO DIVINA

LECTIO

1 Corinthians 13:1-2, 4, 11
Paul wrote his first letter to the Corinthians during the last year of his three-year ministry in Ephesus (in modern-day Turkey), around the spring of 56 A.D. He had established the church in Corinth five years earlier. Since Paul's departure, problems have sprung up: lawsuits, sexual immorality, and doctrinal confusion. Paul writes to address these problems and bring about resolution and unity among the members.

MEDITATIO

What personal message does the text have for me?

ORATIO

What do I say to the Lord in response to His word?

CONTEMPLATIO

What conversion of mind, heart, and life is He asking of me today?

How did I progress in living the Word today?

Friday after Ash Wednesday
REFLECTION

Someone needs you to listen to his or her whole story. There is someone you have cut off, some cue you have missed. Who is that person and how are you going to give him or her they attention God wants you to give to them?

PRAY

Jesus, teach me to listen.
Let me listen the way You do
and help me to hear the nuances
of someone else's heart.

saturday

PHILIPPIANS 4:11-13

Not that I am referring to being in need; for I have learned to be content with whatever I have. I know what it is to have little, and I know what it is to have plenty. In any and all circumstances I have learned the secret of being well-fed and of going hungry, of having plenty and of being in need. I can do all things through him who strengthens me.

FOR FURTHER CONTEMPLATION:

JAMES 1:12-18

C. S. Lewis observed that, "For pride is spiritual cancer: it eats up the very possibility of love, or contentment, or even common sense." (*Mere Christianity*)

I have had cancer. That year of treatment, the time of recovery, the intense fear, and both spiritual darkness and spiritual light make me something of a firsthand witness to the formidable power of cancer. The perception of how much one needs God is intense and that is a blessing, though a painful one.

When one has cancer, rarely is there a thought that isn't held captive by its presence. When one has cancer, all one's time and energy and money is prioritized towards eradicating it. When one has cancer, one is acutely aware of the power it has over life itself. When one has cancer, she doesn't put off until tomorrow the imposing task of cutting it out of her life and healing her body in its aftermath.

Sin is like cancer. It begins small and then, if left unchecked, it permeates every part of our being. No one wants to surrender his or her body to a disease that debilitates and destroys it. Every natural impulse compels us to fight the marauding invader that threatens to rob us of everything we hold most dear. When our bodies are ill, we seek healing.

So it is with our souls. Lent is our time of intense treatment and healing. We look to diagnose what ails our spiritual selves, and to heal the illness of our souls caused by sin. Pride is the root of our sin. It's where the metastases of other deadly sins originate.

During Lent we hear the urgent call to re-prioritize, to excise the sins. Lent is day after day under the loving care of the Great Physician. Our sins cause pain in our lives and in the lives of others. When we confront the pain, and peer closely at the sin, we begin to let the infection of pride bubble under the disinfectant. God will use our pain for His redemptive purpose. Lent can be the healing path back to wholeness in Christ.

As we expose the pathology of pride and we let God's healing grace infuse the virtue needed to eradicate it, we open ourselves to love and to contentment. Much like the treatment of cancer, some days will be difficult. We might feel overwhelmed and alone. Reach out to community on those days; ask for prayer and for the support that comes with just one good friend who can listen. Some days will go more smoothly and we'll be given the grace to see the progress we're making. Take time on those days to record the good and to count the blessings. As you journal your way through this truly beautiful season, begin to notice how God is working within you to heal your soul and also your heart. Praise Him as we see the common sense understanding of God's will and how everything does work together for His good (Romans 8:28), if only we get our ugly sin-disease out of the way.

ELIZABETH FOSS

MUCH LIKE THE
TREATMENT OF CANCER,
SOME DAYS WILL
BE DIFFICULT.
WE MIGHT FEEL
OVERWHELMED AND ALONE.
REACH OUT TO
COMMUNITY ON THOSE DAYS;
ASK FOR PRAYER
AND FOR THE SUPPORT
THAT COMES WITH JUST ONE
GOOD FRIEND WHO
CAN LISTEN.

LECTIO DIVINA

LECTIO

Philippians 4:11-13

Philippians is an epistle of joy. Although St. Paul was imprisoned when he wrote this letter, he writes with optimism to the people of Philippi, located in Macedonia. The Philippians were enduring persecution (most likely from civil authorities), and Paul encourages them to hold fast to Christ and draw strength from Him.

MEDITATIO

What personal message does the text have for me?

ORATIO

What do I say to the Lord in response to His word?

CONTEMPLATIO

What conversion of mind, heart, and life is He asking of me today?

How did I progress in living the Word today?

ACTIO

Saturday after Ash Wednesday
REFLECTION

Take a few moments today to write out your
expectations and your hopes for this season.

PRAY

Jesus, I come to you with good intentions.
I want this to be a fruitful Lent,
one that brings me closer to You,
heals my wounded soul,
and finds me stronger in my faith at Easter.
Open my eyes to your diagnosis
of my soul and grant me
the grace to amend my ways.

first week of lent

EVERY DAY THIS WEEK:

SCRIPTURE READINGS

ESSAY REFLECTION

LECTIO DIVINA

ACTIO REFLECTION

PRAYER

MORE THIS WEEK:

BEGIN WEEKLY SCRIPTURE MEMORY

INTRODUCTION OF LENT ACTIO (PAGE 60)

REPENT, FORGIVE, GIVE THANKS

WEEKLY SCRIPTURE MEMORY

FIRST SUNDAY OF LENT

Here, we begin to memorize Colossians 3:12-17.

Over the course of Lent, we will commit to memory the entire passage Paul gives to the Colossians in order to tell them how to live a new life in the Lord. Taking it just a little bit at a time and building week after week, we can commit the passage to memory and—even better—we can hide it in our hearts.

COLOSSIANS 3:12

AS GOD'S CHOSEN ONES, HOLY AND BELOVED,
CLOTHE YOURSELVES WITH COMPASSION,
KINDNESS, HUMILITY, MEEKNESS, AND PATIENCE.

C·L·O·T·H·E
YOURSELVES
with

compassion,
kindness,
humility,
meekness,
& patience.

COLOSSIANS 3:12

WEEKLY PLANS

SUNDAY

MONDAY

TUESDAY

WEDNESDAY

THURSDAY

FRIDAY

SATURDAY

PRAY + FAST + GIVE

sunday

LUKE 15:11-24

Then Jesus said, "There was a man who had two sons. The younger of them said to his father, 'Father, give me the share of the property that will belong to me.' So he divided his property between them. A few days later the younger son gathered all he had and traveled to a distant country, and there he squandered his property in dissolute living. When he had spent everything, a severe famine took place throughout that country, and he began to be in need. So he went and hired himself out to one of the citizens of that country, who sent him to his fields to feed the pigs. He would gladly have filled himself with the pods that the pigs were eating; and no one gave him anything. But when he came to himself he said, 'How many of my father's hired hands have bread enough and to spare, but here I am dying of hunger! I will get up and go to my father, and I will say to him, "Father, I have sinned against heaven and before you; I am no longer worthy to be called your son; treat me like one of your hired hands."' So he set off and went to his father. But while he was still far off, his father saw him and was filled with compassion; he ran and put his arms around him and kissed him. Then the son said to him, 'Father, I have sinned against heaven and before you; I am no longer worthy to be called your son.' But the father said to his slaves, 'Quickly, bring out a robe—the best one—and put it on him; put a ring on his finger and sandals on his feet. And get the fatted calf and kill it, and let us eat and celebrate; for this son of mine was dead and is alive again; he was lost and is found!' And they began to celebrate."

FOR FURTHER CONTEMPLATION:

PSALM 137:1,4-6

I pondered this devotion as I cleaned up after Thanksgiving dinner. My family gathered in the kitchen, washing dishes and debating the merits of apple pie versus pumpkin pie. It was a very heated debate, but one filled with love and laughter.

Family.

As I cleared the table, I was reminded of this parable of the prodigal son. How many family dinners did the son miss because of his stubbornness and pride? How many tears did his father shed in the quiet of the night wondering where he was and if he was OK?

Thankgsiving evening, as we drove home, I asked my son a question. "Jonathan, when you think of the prodigal son, what comes to mind?" His answer came swift and honest.

"Well, the son has messed up royally. He insulted his father and has basically stolen his inheritance away. It's like he went to Vegas and lost his mind. Then one morning he wakes up on the side of the road, alone and hung over. He is beside himself as every bad choice he has made comes crashing down on him. He wants to go home so badly that he is willing to be a servant in his own home. So he practices his big speech as he finds his way home. Then the most amazing thing happens, his father rushes to meet him. He runs, Mom! Arms open wide. I guess that's the part that's hard for me. I don't think I could do it. Forgive him so easily."

The car was quiet for a few moments, and then my husband entered the conversation. "Jonathan, if you did all the things the prodigal son did in the Gospel, and you chose to finally come home, what do you think your mother and I would do?"

Without a moment's hesitation my son broke me with his response. "You would open the door and let me in. You would have your arms wide open waiting for me to come close. Yep. And Mom would be hysterically crying saying, 'Praise God he is home' or something like that, over and over again. Yep. Arms wide open just like the father in the parable."

Tears slid down my face as I gently held my husband's hand. I did not want my son to see my reaction to his honest and vulnerable response. I was overwhelmed with relief that he knew that, no matter what, he could always come home. That he knew we would be waiting, with arms wide open, to welcome him back into the family fold.

Jonathan continued. "The thing is, the son had to be ready to receive forgiveness. He had to be ready to listen and obey his father. That's the hard part for me. I don't always feel ready to receive."

Ready to receive forgiveness. Oh son, you are not alone there.

How about you, my sisters in Christ? Are you ready to receive forgiveness? What sin resides in your heart that you feel unworthy of this gift? Are you willing to let it go this Lent? God the Father is waiting to meet you in the confessional with arms wide open to give you forgiveness, mercy, and grace. Be confident that when you approach the Father with a humble and contrite heart, whether you feel worthy or not, that He will come running arms wide open to smother you with love and bring you once again into the fold of His household.

We are at the beginning of our Lenten journey, this time of sacrifice, fasting, and reflection. Look to the cross where our Lord Jesus Christ hangs, arms wide open in the ultimate embrace of our sins. There is nothing that stands between you and Him but pride. So lay it down, no matter how long you've carried it or how bad you think it is. Allow Him to love you arms wide open.

MARY LENABURG

ALLOW HIM TO *LOVE YOU* ARMS WIDE OPEN.

LECTIO DIVINA

LECTIO

Luke 15:11-24
Luke's Gospel was written for Gentile Christians, sometime in the 80s A.D. The central theme is the universality of the Good News. This Gospel also stresses the mercy of God; Luke pays special attention to Jesus' merciful works. Because of this emphasis on mercy, it's perhaps unsurprising that the parable of the Prodigal Son is found only in Luke's Gospel.

MEDITATIO

What personal message does the text have for me?

ORATIO

What do I say to the Lord in response to His word?

CONTEMPLATIO

What conversion of mind, heart, and life is He asking of me today?

How did I progress in living the Word today?

ACTIO

First Sunday of Lent
REFLECTION

Describe for yourself what it feels like to be
truly at home with your Father. Detail the peace
of that experience. Can you see the spiritual
beauty of your real self and your real home?
Can you let yourself feel the longing that
comes with exile? Give yourself time to sink
into the deep desire to turn back and go home.

49

PRAY

Father God, I sit by the waters of Babylon and weep.
I want to turn back and go home.
I want to shed the dirty rags of this existence
and put on the fine robe of love that
You hold out for me.
Please help me to repent and return.

monday

LUKE 6:27-31

"But I say to you that listen, Love your enemies, do good to those who hate you, bless those who curse you, pray for those who abuse you. If anyone strikes you on the cheek, offer the other also; and from anyone who takes away your coat do not withhold even your shirt. Give to everyone who begs from you; and if anyone takes away your goods, do not ask for them again. Do to others as you would have them do to you."

FOR FURTHER CONTEMPLATION:

COLOSSIANS 3:12-14

1 PETER 2:19

One thing this Lent calls us to do is to forgive as much as it calls us to repent. As we live out these days, we will take a good hard look at the state of our souls and at the tendency towards sins that challenge us. You can expect an interesting phenomenon to happen here: you will think that you see clearly the sins of other people. You will recognize people in your life in the descriptions of how sin manifests itself.

It's easier to see other people's "sins." Sometimes, we're just seeing the reflections of our own souls. Other times, we do see someone else's sins and we're called to forgive, often without the other person even acknowledging his fault or asking to be forgiven.

In this fallen world, even the people we love act with enmity towards us; they hurt us, falling into the category of people Jesus was talking about when He said, "But I say to you, love your enemies and pray for those who persecute you." (Matthew 5:44)

You can be persecuted right there in your own Christian home. Happens all the time. We are sinners living with sinners.

And Jesus calls us to bless in the mess. "Do not repay evil for evil or abuse for abuse; but, on the contrary, repay with a blessing. It is for this that you were called—that you might inherit a blessing." (1 Peter 3:9)

Later, we'll discuss the fine art of repenting and apologizing, of seeking and granting forgiveness. For now, just know that in the next six weeks, you will see places where you have sinned, but you will also recognize the sins of others. Every day, let go of those sins committed against you and forgive them. If you don't, they'll choke you. Every day, before you turn the page, forgive the sins. Then, hopefully, in God's time, the two of you will have a chance to bring about greater healing.

We will return repeatedly to Saint Paul's words. He calls us to cover one another with love, to remember that "love bears all things, believes all things, hopes all things, endures all things." (1 Corinthians 13:7) When we graciously forgive without being asked, the sin—unrepented—doesn't go away. But it is covered in love and endured with grace.

God enters in. You can't erase the unrepented sin. You can't change the heart of that sinner. All you can do is act in love to bear all things. And that's a lot. Many a marriage has been saved—and even made very happy—because spouses seek the grace to bear all the things.

But God...

God can envelope you in love. He can work in your heart to return good for evil, without being manipulative. He can work in your heart to help you recognize your own culpability. And then, He can give you the grace to truly and fully repent and know His complete forgiveness—the utter obliteration of your sins.

You can't do that for someone else, but you can pray that God will. While you wait for Him to work in someone else's heart, you can know that He is already working in yours, loving your graciousness, delighted to see you extend goodness, even to sinners, especially to sinners. We enter into His passion every time we forgive without asking forgiveness. "When he was abused, he did not return abuse; when he suffered, he did not threaten; but he entrusted himself to the one who judges justly." (1 Peter 2:23)

God knows the sins of other people that hurt you. Maybe it's time to surrender them to Him? God understands your pain and He is ministering to it right now. Let that be enough. Take His crown of thorns upon your own head, know it pierced Him for your sins, but know also that He felt the pain of the sins that hurt you.

And He chose to shoulder the cross for them: to put on that heavy load—love rough-hewn from heavy timber—so that you can forgive and bear all things and He can forgive and truly make them new.

A NOTE ABOUT JOURNALING:

For the next few weeks, take the time at the end of the reflection to closely examine how certain sins manifest themselves in your life. We hope you'll give this step ample time and prayer. We have given you space on the actio page to remind yourself to repent, to forgive, and to give thanks.

ELIZABETH FOSS

LECTIO DIVINA

Luke 6:27-31

Luke's focus on mercy continues today in his recounting of the Beatitudes. In today's verses, Jesus is speaking to his disciples and the large crowd that has gathered to hear Him speak. Jesus tells the crowd not to extend mercy only to those who love them, but to enemies as well.

MEDITATIO

What personal message does the text have for me?

ORATIO

What do I say to the Lord in response to His word?

CONTEMPLATIO

What conversion of mind, heart, and life is He asking of me today?

How did I progress in living the Word today?

ACTIO

How will I make my life a gift for others in charity?
What does God want me to do today?

REPENT

Have I held past hurts tightly within myself and refused to let go of the hurt, the anger, or the pain?

FORGIVE

Is there someone against whom you've held out forgiveness, some past grievance that might take some work to relinquish? Can you offer this Lent for the intention of completely forgiving?

GIVE THANKS

For the times that forgiveness has been offered to you swiftly and freely, give thanks.

PRAY

Forgiveness is not easy, Lord.
I clench the hurt tightly in my fists and hold on.
Why? I am afraid. I fear the vulnerability that comes
with letting down my guard and letting go.
Let Your spirit of forgiveness live in me.
Please, help me to forgive.

tuesday

ISAIAH 57:15

For thus says the high and lofty one
   who inhabits eternity, whose name is Holy:
I dwell in the high and holy place,
   and also with those who are contrite and
humble in spirit,
to revive the spirit of the humble,
   and to revive the heart of the contrite.

FOR FURTHER CONTEMPLATION:

---

1 CORINTHIANS 4:7

ISAIAH 66:2

PSALM 138:6

Do you ever feel like your heart is crushed, day after day? Like you know you want to live in step with God and to pursue all that is holy, but the stuff of everyday life just keeps coming at you with such relentless precision that you just can't?

You begin the day with the best of intentions and you're trying with all your might, but almost inevitably, the wheels fall off. You can't keep your peace. You can't keep your patience. You can't keep your wits about you.

That's right. You can't.

Lent is all about returning to the God who can. Lent is about trading your false sense of security for His enduring, authentic peace, your feeble attempts to refrain from blowing it for His ability to calm every storm, and your dimly-lit understanding for His mastery of the entire universe.

Lent is about becoming more like Him.

In order to become more like Him, we have to humbly admit that we are nothing without Him. Those days where we just can't get it together despite our very best efforts are the days that remind us that we need God desperately. Those are the days that can give birth to humility if we let them.

With the grace of God, let them.

Humility is a holy guide who leads us through the desert of those days. Humility will stir in us a hunger for God in His word, and open our hearts wide to the Holy Spirit who can make us entirely new creations. It is humility that brings us near to the Lord who hangs, naked and split open, on the cross.

Sometimes, we get so caught up in the rhythm of the workplace or the one-up song of social media that we think we have to be successful by the standards of the world. We might even think that those standards are how we will find happiness at last. Those worldly accomplishments are very likely to make us proud.

But God only knows the proud from afar.

He keeps His distance from the ones who are striving so to keep up with their neighbors. He does. They are not close to Him and that's a hefty price to pay for worldly acclaim.

He is intimate with the lowly. He dwells in the contrite. When we understand that we are powerless to be virtuous without Him, and when we know that virtue is true success, we open ourselves to His riches.

It is God who helps you keep your peace. It is Christ who imbues a spirit of patience within you. It is the Holy Spirit who replaces our scattered witlessness with His wisdom.

Humility is greatness in God's economy.

ELIZABETH FOSS

LENT IS ABOUT BECOMING MORE LIKE HIM.

LECTIO DIVINA

LECTIO

Isaiah 57:15
Isaiah received his call to prophecy around 742 B.C. when he was 20 years old. His mission spanned from around 741 B.C.- 701 B.C. in Jerusalem. He worked during a period of immense political and social upheaval. Isaiah is also the most frequently-quoted prophet in the New Testament. Today's reading continues Isaiah's theme of restoration and hope that began in chapter 55.

MEDITATIO

What personal message does the text have for me?

ORATIO

What do I say to the Lord in response to His word?

CONTEMPLATIO

What conversion of mind, heart, and life is He asking of me today?

How did I progress in living the Word today?

ACTIO

How will I make my life a gift for others in charity?
What does God want me to do today?

REPENT

Did you lose your patience today because you thought what you were doing was more important than the person who interrupted you?

Did you try to figure out a problem on your own, forgetting to ask God for His direction before even attempting to discern the path forward?

Are you puffed up by accolades of this world?

Do you set your goals according to what lofty award or promotion or grad school admission you want to attain, failing to discern if those are God's goals for you?

FORGIVE

Did someone snub you? Lay it at the foot of the cross.

GIVE THANKS

Did you kneel down and tie a shoe, stop what you were doing to offer a drink, let someone ahead of you in line because your time is really not more important than hers ?
Did you bow low to the presence of God in your friends and neighbors?

PRAY

You are the Master of the Universe,
mighty and powerful and omniscient.
Please remind me that it is in You
and You alone that I want to live
and breathe and have my being.
Please make me increasingly aware
of Your goals for me and
Your intentions for how I should
spend my time.
Let me walk in
step with You.

wednesday

JEREMIAH 17:9-10

The heart is devious above all else;
  it is perverse—
  who can understand it?
I the Lord test the mind
  and search the heart,
to give to all according to their ways,
  according to the fruit of their doings.

FOR FURTHER CONTEMPLATION:

PROVERBS 3:5-7

Your heart is devious and it is perverse.

God is not deceived; He sees straight into your heart every time. Scary thought, isn't it? There is Someone who knows. God knows everything: every thought and every impulse, good or bad.

There's more.

We think we know ourselves. We tend to the task of knowing ourselves. We can be so self-absorbed with what's in our heads and what we think we need that we nurture our sense of self with more consistency than we nurture those in our care.

We half-listen to our children, never taking our eyes from the screen.

We hear our friends share their hearts, but our heads have already moved on to our stories, which we share too eagerly before giving careful considerations to theirs.

We hurt people when we are self-absorbed. We break them when we put our own agenda before their cries. We injure the very people God has entrusted to our care when we choose ourselves over them in a million seemingly little ways. Ultimately, we alienate ourselves from them and from God. These are the fruits of our doings.

We fall into the lonely hole of our own navel-gazing, and pretty soon we are also choosing to wallow and to puzzle and to work out on our own the myriad complexities He lets this life offer us. He sees them. He knows them. He wants them to be the path to Him. But we are so self-absorbed with the map of our making that we miss the journey He keeps inviting us to take.

The journey with Him.

God doesn't want you to figure it out. He wants you to lean on Him. He doesn't want you to keep incessantly clicking through Google, questing after the most current morsel of irrelevant knowledge because you are afraid of missing out on the world's latest and greatest. Deep down, you think you are one click away from being satisfied. And happy. One click to happy.

That's not how this works.

Unless you're clicking on His word, you are not growing closer to contentment. Or happiness, or genuine joy. Indeed, you might be unintentionally sowing seeds of discontent with your restless pursuits.

Saint Augustine offers timeless wisdom, as relevant in the digital age as it was when it was first published in 397 AD:

> *Thou hast made us*
> *for thyself, O Lord,*
> *and our heart*
> *is restless*
> *until it finds*
> *its rest in thee.*

God wants you to spend time with Him, to know Him and to trust Him and to ask Him at least as often as you ask Google: Which way do I go? What would you have me know?

ELIZABETH FOSS

LECTIO DIVINA

LECTIO

Jeremiah 17:9-10
Jeremiah was a priest from the town of Anathoth near Jerusalem. His writings discuss the last days of the Kingdom of Judah and foretell the destruction of Jerusalem and the Temple, as well as the founding of a new covenant in Messianic times. In today's passage, Jeremiah speaks about people who place their trust in outward things and individual strength, instead of in the Lord.

MEDITATIO

What personal message does the text have for me?

ORATIO

What do I say to the Lord in response to His word?

CONTEMPLATIO

What conversion of mind, heart, and life is He asking of me today?

How did I progress in living the Word today?

ACTIO

How will I make my life a gift for others in charity?
What does God want me to do today?

REPENT

Do you fail to give your full attention to people when they are talking to you?

Do you spend too much time in front of screens?

Do you spend more time on social media than you do in the Word of God?

Do you think more of book smarts than you do of knowledge of the nature of God?

FORGIVE

Does someone only half-listen when you talk to him?

Give it to Jesus, who hears your every whisper.

GIVE THANKS

Were you able to pull your eyes away from your screens today and look into the eyes of someone you love?

Did you spend time with Jesus today and listen to Him more than you talked to Him?

Did you spend time with a friend today and listen more than you talked to her?

PRAY

God and Creator,
help me to be aware that You
made me in Your image.
Your vision of me is who I am at my core,
and when I live that vision,
I will be truly content in my own skin.
Tune my heart to Yours, Lord.
Teach me to know that I am
nothing without You and
everything that matters with You.

thursday

JAMES 4:6-7

But he gives all the more grace; therefore it
says, "God opposes the proud, but gives grace
to the humble." Submit yourselves therefore
to God. Resist the devil, and he will flee from
you.

FOR FURTHER CONTEMPLATION:

---

1 PETER 5:5-7

DEUTERONOMY 31:6

Recently, sins from my past began to haunt me once again. I met with my confessor several times over a period of a few months, and each time, I'd rattle off those old sins. Some I re-confessed because I'd fallen back into bad habits. But most of them I just couldn't forget. Despite repeating the act of contrition multiple times and being given absolution, I worried that I was somehow an exception to the story of God's great mercy.

Finally, the priest hearing my confession asked me point-blank if I thought my sins were bigger than God's forgiveness. I didn't know what to say. So with great kindness, the priest explained that holding on to my sins—believing that they were too big for even God to forgive—was actually a form of pride.

Pride? Here I'd thought I was being humble, envisioning myself little, weak, and so sinful that I needed to re-confess the same things over and over. But I had fallen for the lie that my sins were bigger than God's willingness to forgive. Rather than trusting in God's grace, I relied on my own judgment as to whether I was worthy of His forgiveness.

Once I realized that pride was at the root of my inability to accept God's grace, I realized that it was also the source of so many of my other sins, especially my tendency to let worry rule my life. When facing difficulties in the past, I saw myself as a little girl raging against an enormous storm. Even before the storm actually got bigger, I imagined it growing as I worried about each and every possible terrible outcome. And as the storm got bigger in my mind, I grew smaller and smaller.

Yet, though we may be little and weak in comparison to obstacles we face, God is neither of those things. And when we let Him in, we can find strength to overcome anything that we face, or any worry about over what we might face in the future. When we let Him provide the protection and refuge He so longs to give us, we actually grow bigger and stronger against the storms in our lives—not because of our own strength, but because of His.

When pride is the hidden root of our anxiety, we believe that we are submitting to God, but we are not, because deep down, we doubt that God is truly stronger than what troubles us. We doubt that, despite our sinfulness, we're truly forgiven and worthy of His help. We might even doubt that He sees us at all. These are lies, whispered by the devil, that distance us from God.

What brings us back to God is trusting in the truth found in His holy word: God does see us, for we are His beloved children. When we come to Him with contrition, we are forgiven. And He is stronger than anything we could ever face. He alone can take what is fearful, anxious, weak, and timid in us and make it strong and bold through His grace.

We must only leave room in our hearts for Him to work. For when we fill ourselves with worry, we leave no space for God. But when we trust that His forgiveness is bigger than our sins, and that His protection is more powerful than our struggles, we can receive the grace and favor He offers us. And that grace helps us answer the call to become the people we were meant to be: bold, strong, and courageous, with God at our side.

ALLISON MCGINLEY

WHEN WE LET HIM PROVIDE THE PROTECTION AND REFUGE HE SO LONGS TO GIVE US, WE ACTUALLY GROW BIGGER AND STRONGER AGAINST THE STORMS IN OUR LIVES—NOT BECAUSE OF OUR OWN STRENGTH, BUT BECAUSE OF HIS.

LECTIO DIVINA

LECTIO

James 4:6-7

James is the first of the "catholic epistles", meaning they appear to be addressed to the whole church, and to not any specific city. James, a cousin of Jesus, probably wrote this letter between 49-62 A.D. The letter focuses on the challenges facing Christians as they live in the pagan world. Today's verses follow James' warning that friendship with the world leads to being set at odds with God.

MEDITATIO

What personal message does the text have for me?

ORATIO

What do I say to the Lord in response to His word?

CONTEMPLATIO

What conversion of mind, heart, and life is He asking of me today?

How did I progress in living the Word today?

ACTIO

How will I make my life a gift for others in charity?
What does God want me to do today?

REPENT

Do you try to play God by worrying excessively?

Are you letting fear crowd out faith?

FORGIVE

Forgive yourself today. Forgive that you make fear bigger than faith.

Give it to the Father who forgives you with gladness.

GIVE THANKS

Did God deliver you from something you fear?

Did He show you how your worries were needless?

PRAY

I will tell You today, Lord,
all the things that worry me, all my fears.
And then, with Your help,
I will leave them at the foot of Your cross.
You are the master of the universe, not me.
You know best how to untangle
all the knots of my life.
I trust You; please increase my trust.

friday

"Woe to you, scribes and Pharisees, hypocrites! For you tithe mint, dill, and cummin, and have neglected the weightier matters of the law: justice and mercy and faith. It is these you ought to have practiced without neglecting the others. You blind guides! You strain out a gnat but swallow a camel!

"Woe to you, scribes and Pharisees, hypocrites! For you clean the outside of the cup and of the plate, but inside they are full of greed and self-indulgence. You blind Pharisee! First clean the inside of the cup, so that the outside also may become clean.

"Woe to you, scribes and Pharisees, hypocrites! For you are like whitewashed tombs, which on the outside look beautiful, but inside they are full of the bones of the dead and of all kinds of filth. So you also on the outside look righteous to others, but inside you are full of hypocrisy and lawlessness.

"Woe to you, scribes and Pharisees, hypocrites! For you build the tombs of the prophets and decorate the graves of the righteous, and you say, 'If we had lived in the days of our ancestors, we would not have taken part with them in shedding the blood of the prophets.' Thus you testify against yourselves that you are descendants of those who murdered the prophets. Fill up, then, the measure of your ancestors. You snakes, you brood of vipers! How can you escape being sentenced to hell?"

FOR FURTHER CONTEMPLATION:

ISAIAH 65:2-5

LUKE 12:1

FIRST WEEK OF LENT

You think you are better than they are. You go about your day, full of such enlightenment and so many lofty ideals, and you think you are too sacred for the regular, everyday people you meet. You do all the right things according to your principles for upright living, and you look down your nose at the people who don't.

You are a hypocrite. And Jesus is very worried about your soul.

Hypocrisy is a cunning, creeping vice. I think it often begins with a child who is taught that it is very important to care about what the neighbors think. That child learns that her value rests in the opinions of others and she grows into a well-intentioned people-pleaser who gets a little dose of Christianity and thinks that if she just does all the right things, so all the right people can check her good behavior on the Good Christian Checklist, she's set for life. And eternity.

In reality, she is merely sowing seeds of self-love and watering them with hypocrisy. Some of us are wired with the desire to impress others, to make them believe the careful illusion that we are something we're not.

If you are blessed with children, know that they can see right through the hypocrisy façade. They know a fake who tells the world one thing and hisses another in anger and impatience at home. And they will reject your God with disgust at the first opportunity. God doesn't ask you to be a perfect parent (or spouse or friend), but He does want you to be an honest one. When you commit sins of hypocrisy—when you say you love God but act like you love your own selfish sins more—you have to acknowledge that and you have to ask forgiveness, even from your children. Especially from your children.

Hypocrisy cares more about what the crowd thinks and not very much about what God knows. Our best guard against hypocrisy is to lean hard into Christ's strong shoulders. Trust Him every day in His word; let Him show you your sins and let Him speak His truth to your heart. Do the hard work of repenting and replacing sin with virtue. Make it genuine. When you start to fake a life of faith when you're around Christian community, you're sliding down that slippery slope into hypocrisy.

Look how many times Jesus says, "Woe to you!" Woe.

Whoa.

Just stop. Stop trying to impress other people. Stop living according to the checklist, even the checklist of seemingly perfect Christians. (Chances are good there's a hefty dose of woe there, too.) Start living in the freedom of Christ.

Stop. Step around the woe. You don't have to please anyone but God. You are accountable only to Him. And He loves you. In all humility, bow your head and ask Him how He would have you act with a genuine, Christlike heart.

ELIZABETH FOSS

AND
HE LOVES
YOU.

LECTIO DIVINA

LECTIO

Matthew 23:23-33
This Gospel was written by the apostle Matthew, between 50-100 A.D. Matthew stresses that Christ is the fulfillment of the Old Testament Scriptures. The Gospel is organized around Jesus' major discourses and actions. These work together to reveal the true nature of His identity and mission. In today's verses, Jesus is speaking to the crowds and his disciples about the hypocrisy of the religious leaders.

MEDITATIO

What personal message does the text have for me?

ORATIO

What do I say to the Lord in response to His word?

CONTEMPLATIO

What conversion of mind, heart, and life is He asking of me today?

How did I progress in living the Word today?

ACTIO

How will I make my life a gift for others in charity?
What does God want me to do today?

REPENT

Do you think that what the crowd thinks, or even what just one person thinks, matters more than what God thinks? Do you act like you do?

Are you a people-pleaser who tries too hard to make everyone like her to the detriment of her own self-worth?

Do you pretend to be a devout Christian, all the while sinning silently inside your head?

FORGIVE

Are there people in your life who taught you that it's very important to keep up appearances?

Forgive them and take your cues from your Creator instead.

GIVE THANKS

Are there Godly examples in your life who speak to your heart with genuine Christlike goodness and show you that looking perfect isn't what it's all about?

Were you able to let go of pretense and just be content in the presence of God today?

PRAY

Dear Jesus, I try so hard. So hard.
But over and over again, I fall short
of my own expectations for myself.
Help me to understand deep down that
You love me for the real me and not for the me
who pretends to have it all together,
or for the me who strives to be perfect.
Help me to see that You have nothing
but compassion for that struggling,
stumbling me, and that You want nothing
more than for me to fully collapse into
Your care and surrender my
will to Your better plan.

ABOVE ALL | FIRST WEEK OF LENT

saturday

"Do not judge, so that you may not be judged. For with the judgment you make you will be judged, and the measure you give will be the measure you get. Why do you see the speck in your neighbor's eye, but do not notice the log in your own eye? Or how can you say to your neighbor, 'Let me take the speck out of your eye,' while the log is in your own eye? You hypocrite, first take the log out of your own eye, and then you will see clearly to take the speck out of your neighbor's eye."

FOR FURTHER CONTEMPLATION:

PROVERBS 21:2

LUKE 16:15

When we look to God's word for rules to live by, it's a good idea to read on. If we stop too soon, we miss the point. If we read, "Do not judge, so that you may not be judged" and stop there, we miss our favorite carpenter's exaggerated illustration of how ridiculous it is to try to correct someone else's faults while remaining ignorantly sinful ourselves.

Jesus warns us that we can't judge the state of another's soul. We can't know how God sees them. Only God can do that. We can, and should, endeavor to walk alongside our neighbors and to lift the load of sin from the burdens they carry if we are able. Pointing out another person's sin should be a personal, intimate act of mercy. This means from the outset that the humble person doesn't trumpet someone else's failings. It also means that when we undertake the difficult task of helping another to see sin, we do it with delicacy and empathy. "Blessed are the merciful, for they will receive mercy." (Matthew 5:7)

The Lord will judge you as you have judged others. Remember that as you expose sins to the light of day and pronounce your own decree. The Lord will be gracious with you; be gracious with your neighbor, both in his presence and behind his back. Pray that the longer you live, the more the Lord will soften your heart to the struggles of other people and open your capacity for empathy. We want to understand the pain behind the sins of other people, and to extend to them the grace and mercy we know in Christ. We also want to love them enough to call them on true sin and to help them remove that speck from their eyes.

Have you ever done that? Taken a speck out of the eye of another? I'm a mom with lots of kids and I've had lots of opportunities to do the delicate work of finding the eyelash or the stray sweater fuzz. It requires good eyes, a steady hand, and equal amounts of patience and gentleness. There is no way to get the speck if I rush in and crash around. And there's no way I could do it with a log in my own eye. For starters, the mere size of the log wouldn't let me get close enough.

Whether we are trying to correct our children or our roommates or our spouses or people we pass on the street, first we have to apply sincere humility to our own logs. We need to know our own sins and the heart behind those sins before we look at someone else's. And we need to be intimate enough and trusted enough by that person to get close enough to see the speck. Then, we go gently with sensitivity and compassion.

Jesus doesn't randomly choose eyes for this example. He very deliberately calls to mind the delicate windows into our souls. He knows that if we do this the wrong way—if we proceed to remove the speck without care and skill—we can do more damage than the speck did. Judging unfairly or without proper gravity or without care to preserve the person's dignity can push them further from the Healer.

Remember, commenting on someone else's sins should be careful, not casual, and it is absolutely critical to the health of your eye and your neighbor's eye that you take care of the log before you begin. Jesus calls to examine our own failings first and move them out of the way, to clear the vision that was clouded by our sin. No one wants a person who can't see clearly messing with her eyes. Also, be sure the speck you're seeing isn't a reflection. So often, it's easy to see the sins we hate most about ourselves in the speech and actions of someone else. Be slow to judge others and quick to judge yourself, then remember the gentleness of removing the speck with delicacy and care.

ELIZABETH FOSS

REMEMBER THE GENTLENESS OF REMOVING THE SPECK WITH DELICACY AND CARE.

LECTIO DIVINA

LECTIO

Matthew 7:1-5
Today's passage from Matthew is part of the Sermon on the Mount, which crystallizes the ideal of the Christian life. Throughout Matthew's Gospel, the apostle shows how Jesus established a new law, one that goes beyond the demands of Mosaic law and calls for deeply interior holiness and brotherly love. Today's verses are an excellent example of how to put this brotherly love into action.

MEDITATIO

What personal message does the text have for me?

ORATIO

What do I say to the Lord in response to His word?

CONTEMPLATIO

What conversion of mind, heart, and life is He asking of me today?

How did I progress in living the Word today?

ACTIO

How will I make my life a gift for others in charity?
What does God want me to do today?

REPENT

Are you quick to judge other people and find them lacking?

Do you make quick, critical assessments of others without considering them with empathy?

Do you criticize harshly or without mercy?

FORGIVE

Does someone judge you hastily and harshly and crush your spirit with awkward recriminations?

Forgive them that sin and know that Jesus looks on you from the cross, with love.

GIVE THANKS

Is there someone in your life who offers gentle guidance to help you see your faults without crushing your spirit?

Are you able to extend that same patient gentleness to the people you love, even if imperfectly?

PRAY

God, when I am tempted to criticize,
slow me down. Help me to see
if it might be my own sin that is the problem.
And when I do have good reason
to help someone else know her sins,
let me gentle and merciful and kind.

second week of lent

EVERY DAY THIS WEEK:

SCRIPTURE READINGS

ESSAY REFLECTION

LECTIO DIVINA

REPENT, FORGIVE, GIVE THANKS

PRAYER

MORE THIS WEEK:

WEEKLY SCRIPTURE MEMORY

WEEKLY SCRIPTURE MEMORY

SECOND SUNDAY OF LENT

Here, we continue to memorize Colossians 3:12-17

Over the course of Lent, we will commit to memory the entire passage Paul gives to the Colossians in order to tell them how to live a new life in the Lord. Taking it just a little bit at a time and building week after week, we can commit the passage to memory and—even better—we can hide it in our hearts.

COLOSSIANS 3:13

BEAR WITH ONE ANOTHER AND, IF ANYONE HAS A
COMPLAINT AGAINST ANOTHER, FORGIVE EACH OTHER;
JUST AS THE LORD HAS FORGIVEN YOU,
SO YOU ALSO MUST FORGIVE.

Bear with one another & forgive each other.

COLOSSIANS 3:13

WEEKLY PLANS

SUNDAY

MONDAY

TUESDAY

WEDNESDAY

THURSDAY

FRIDAY

SATURDAY

PRAY - FAST - GIVE

sunday

HEBREWS 4:4-10

For in one place it speaks about the seventh day as follows, "And God rested on the seventh day from all his works." And again in this place it says, "They shall not enter my rest." Since therefore it remains open for some to enter it, and those who formerly received the good news failed to enter because of disobedience, again he sets a certain day—"today"—saying through David much later, in the words already quoted,

"Today, if you hear his voice,
do not harden your hearts."

For if Joshua had given them rest, God would not speak later about another day. So then, a sabbath rest still remains for the people of God; for those who enter God's rest also cease from their labors as God did from his.

FOR FURTHER CONTEMPLATION:

PSALM 127:2

ROMANS 4:5

SECOND WEEK OF LENT

I sat down with my daughter after she awoke from her nap. Her body eased against mine. Immediately, I felt my pulse drop, my body relax, my mind slow down. Something about her close presence was calming.

This phenomenon is common. A child comes to us full of anxiety because of a scrape to the knee. With a simple kiss to the affected area, the pain is eased. An extended embrace from a loved one when we're suffering from acute grief will often bring about visible relief. A warm caress to the forehead when we're down with the flu is soothing in the midst of discomfort.

There is something about loving presence that causes us to relax.

But, on the flip side of the coin, without relaxation, we lose our ability to be present. Dare I say, to love.

Much of the day we go about our work, not wanting to put it down until the last box is checked off on the to-do list. It is easy to slip into a cycle whereby we eat, breathe, sleep by that list. We can let it rule our lives. We can become so concerned with making sure it all gets done, that we walk straight into the lie that our worth is tied up with getting it all accomplished.

When this happens, we are no longer present to the truth about ourselves. We have a hard time being receptively present to those around us. And we allow God's presence to fade into the background.

We have lost sight of being God's instrument, but rather have tried to usurp the role that belongs to Him alone. We attempt to carry the weight of the world on our shoulders when Someone Else already carried it in the form of a cross.

We were made for rest. Toil is a result of the Fall. Our final destination is a place of eternal rest.

On Sundays, in a special way, we are called to remember and practice living this state of being the Lord calls us to. We go to Mass. In that place, we catch a glimpse behind the veil where the communion of saints rest in His presence. We are drawn up into the eschaton, reminded of where we are headed and for what, or rather Whom, we should be living. We carry this back to our homes, leaning into the Sabbath day, enjoying the presence of our loved ones, and refreshing ourselves for the work week ahead.

Do not let this practice go as you race about your week. Pause for true moments of rest —for God, for yourself, for others. It is what will carry you through. It is where you will discover peace. It is where you will find, above all, love.

LAUREL MUFF

PAUSE FOR TRUE MOMENTS OF REST —FOR GOD, FOR YOURSELF, FOR OTHERS. IT IS WHAT WILL CARRY YOU THROUGH. IT IS WHERE YOU WILL DISCOVER PEACE. IT IS WHERE YOU WILL FIND, *ABOVE ALL, LOVE.*

LECTIO DIVINA

LECTIO

Hebrews 4:4-10
Written before the fall of Jerusalem to the Romans in 70 A.D., we don't know who the author is, or who the intended audience was. Hebrews focuses on the priesthood and sacrifice of Christ, as well as how the New Covenant is infinitely superior to the previous covenants God made in the Old Testament. Today's verses focus on how, even under the New Covenant, God still commands that His people rest on the Sabbath.

MEDITATIO

What personal message
does the text have for me?

ORATIO

What do I say to the Lord in
response to His word?

CONTEMPLATIO

What conversion of mind,
heart, and life is He asking
of me today?

How did I progress in living the Word today?

ACTIO

How will I make my life a gift for others in charity?
What does God want me to do today?

REPENT

Do you miss Mass because the schedule crowds it out?
Do you miss Mass because you've filled the rest of the week so full that you're too tired to get out of bed on Sunday morning?
Do you fail to spend your Sundays genuinely worshipping and resting?
Do you worry too much about "wasting" time and so work needlessly on Sundays, forgetting that God is the master of time and He has commanded you to rest?

FORGIVE

Does someone push you relentlessly on Sundays, asking you to forego rest for productivity? Forgive that sin and rest with the Savior who knew how to rest.

GIVE THANKS

What fills you, restores you, brings you deep rest? Make a list of ways to truly rest and then consult it frequently, committing to bring those ideas to life in order be sustained by God, who provides restful opportunities for you and commands you to take them.

PRAY

Thank You for the gift of Sunday.
Thank You for insisting that I stop and truly rest.
Help me to honor this day with my heart and with my body.
Please, Lord, surround me with people who
will enter into Your rest with me today.
Help us all to put work away and to allow
You the time and space to
heal and restore us.

monday

ZECHARIAH 7:11-13

But they refused to listen, and turned a
stubborn shoulder, and stopped their ears
so as not to hear. They made their hearts
adamant in order not to hear the law and the
words that the LORD of hosts had sent by his
spirit through the former prophets. Therefore
great wrath came from the LORD of hosts.
Just as, when I called they would not hear, so,
when they called, I would not hear, says the
LORD of hosts...

FOR FURTHER CONTEMPLATION:

PROVERBS 1:23-24 (see especially the NABRE translation)

PROVERBS 29:1

1 PETER 2:23

Pride is tricky, devious, and deceptive. Sometimes we are suffering at the hands of pride and we have no idea that's the true problem. For instance, pride is often at the root of extreme sensitivity that shows itself in defensiveness.

This prideful behavior isn't all puffed up and arrogant-looking. Instead, it cowers a bit; it cringes at the mention of its faults. Maybe it cries at the drop of a hat. It seems so weak and tender that it could be confused with humility. (If, indeed, humility were weak, but it's not, right?)

Humility is the genuine understanding that we are nothing without God. When we are truly in step with the Lord, humility is the scaffolding upon which we build our lives, and it's the firm foundation of truth for our genuinely Christian behavior. We know that it is God who makes us good and God who succeeds through us, so we refuse to buy into the lie that we are greater than we are.

But the lie whispers. And even the very sensitive person—maybe especially the very sensitive person—hears the lie. Her sense of self-worth is built upon the shaky foundation that she has to be good enough, better than everyone else, under her own power. When she's challenged by a criticism or rebuke, she's knocked from the tentative platform of her own fragile self-esteem into the utter despair and fear of failing that quickly shows itself as defensiveness.

She's trapped in this never-ending pattern of working so hard under her own power to be better, to succeed—making herself larger and larger in her own mind, under her own efforts—until she learns that she has limits, and, even worse, faults. Finally, she becomes utterly disappointed and disgusted with herself. Instead of pausing there, and seeing the faults for what they are, listening to wise reproof, and understanding how the way out is a teachable spirit, she is stubborn and sticks her fingers in her ears. She cannot bear to hear that she isn't perfect.

The pattern repeats again and again, until, exhausted by the effort, she loses faith, cannot trust even a little in the power of the God who created her, and feels she is beyond healing.

Pride has killed her, all because her exaggerated sensitivity made her unwilling to open herself to constructive criticism and the grace of salvation.

It's a true story.

But it doesn't have to end that way.

Humility hears reproof, listens carefully with an open heart, takes it to the Lord in prayer, and asks Him to shed divine light on it, to show her where the truth is. And then, humility allows her to hand the sin to God, continuing on in good faith, trusting that the Lord will care tenderly for her soul, granting her the grace to genuinely root out the tangles of sin and let the goodness flourish in fertile ground.

ELIZABETH FOSS

THE LORD WILL CARE TENDERLY FOR HER SOUL, GRANTING HER THE GRACE TO GENUINELY ROOT OUT THE TANGLES OF SIN AND LET THE GOODNESS FLOURISH IN FERTILE GROUND

LECTIO DIVINA

LECTIO

Zechariah 7:11-13
Zechariah is one of the 12 minor prophets. Composed around 520 B.C., Zechariah encouraged the people in their faith after the Babylonian Exile and the rebuilding of the Temple. He called on the people to recognize their own failings, repent of their sins, and place their trust in a merciful God. In these verses, God states His desire for a relationship with His people, but they are stubborn and reject His invitation.

MEDITATIO

What personal message does the text have for me?

ORATIO

What do I say to the Lord in response to His word?

CONTEMPLATIO

What conversion of mind, heart, and life is He asking of me today?

How did I progress in living the Word today?

ACTIO

How will I make my life a gift for others in charity?

What does God want me to do today?

REPENT

Is defensiveness your first reaction to criticism?

Do you cower and weep or lash out in anger at the suggestion you could be wrong?

FORGIVE

You've offered gentle and sincere reproof and it's been met with denial and defensiveness. You are frustrated and saddened because the relationship is stuck in a no-growth pattern. Forgive this upside down manifestation of pride. Lay it at the feet of the Savior and ask Him to soften hearts and make them vulnerable to gentle correction.

GIVE THANKS

Is there someone in your life who cares enough to lovingly show you your weaknesses?

PRAY

Dear Lord, I want to be good.
I try so hard to be good at everything I do.
And I'm struck to my core every time
my "good" isn't good enough.
Help me to see Your good for me,
to understand that what I really want is to be holy.
And help me to soften my heart
when I hear Godly reproof and to accept
its message with humility.

tuesday

GALATIANS 6:3-5

―――――――

For if those who are nothing think they are something, they deceive themselves. All must test their own work; then that work, rather than their neighbor's work, will become a cause for pride. For all must carry their own loads.

FOR FURTHER CONTEMPLATION:

―――――――

2 CORINTHIANS 10:12

MICAH 6:8

Arms spread wide, side pierced, body battered and bloodied, He hangs for us. Why?

Not so that we can make partner. Not so that we can write a bestselling book. Not so that someone can attach a title of distinction to our name.

He does not hang to satisfy our ambition.

He hangs so that we can live with Him forever in heaven.

He hangs so that we can love Him well here on earth. And in order to do that, we have to walk humbly with Him. Can we keep up–in humility—with Someone who poured Himself out on a cross? Not even a little, really, but it is our privilege to spend our lifetimes trying.

It is not a sin to want do our best. We should work wholeheartedly. That whole heart, though, belongs to God. If our sense of what our best is rests upon the evaluations of other people, pride is what is driving us, not a humble commitment to living the vocation to which He calls us.

Measuring ourselves against any other standard but our Lord's humble service is a two-edged sword. One lethal side is the devaluation of our own worth. The other is the devaluation of our neighbor. Often, when we judge ourselves according to titles and accolades, we judge our neighbor similarly. God calls us to a different standard than the culture's standard. Submission to God's standard excludes our arrogance. We stop seeing people as the sum total of their resumes and start understanding that the attributes of God can't be quantified or titled.

God calls some people to wealth and influence and fame. For those people, living a life of merciful humility will be even more difficult. It is so difficult that three of the four Gospels remind us that it is easier for a camel to go through the eye of a needle than for a rich man to enter the kingdom of God. (Matthew 19:24, Mark 10:25, Luke 18:25)

In her arrogance, the proud person wants power. She puts herself above other people and looks down on those who have lesser value in the world's economy of prestige.

And then she worries that she, too, lacks sufficient power and prestige. There is a constant, ceaseless jostling for position and affirmation, a constant, creeping anxiety that keeps whispering "never enough."

Walking humbly with God calls us to a simpler place. It allows us to be content with faithful obscurity, trusting that He can use us well wherever He calls us, with whomever He chooses. Humility allows us to trust that God will do great things with our small offerings. Further, humility helps us to understand that God's idea of greatness differs from the world's idea of greatness, and that God's greatness is deeply satisfying and eternally valuable. It's not capricious. It doesn't twist in the winds of change. And God's greatness—the greatness to which He calls you and me? It's peaceful. There's no worry attached to it.

Imagine that? Peaceful contentment in being the best that God calls us to be.

ELIZABETH FOSS

HE HANGS
SO THAT
WE CAN LIVE
WITH HIM
FOREVER IN
HEAVEN.

LECTIO DIVINA

LECTIO

Galatians 6:3-5

Paul wrote this letter to the people of Galatia (in modern-day Turkey) in the early 50s A.D. The letter was written to counteract false theology that was spreading throughout the region. It is Paul's most intense epistle and demonstrates how the Gospel message works practically in day-to-day life. In today's passage, Paul reminds his readers that they must examine their own lives and not compare them with others. Every person is responsible for his own actions before God.

MEDITATIO

What personal message does the text have for me?

ORATIO

What do I say to the Lord in response to His word?

CONTEMPLATIO

What conversion of mind, heart, and life is He asking of me today?

How did I progress in living the Word today?

ACTIO

How will I make my life a gift for others in charity?
What does God want me to do today?

REPENT

Are you living according to the world's economy or God's?

Do you consider someone worth your time and attention only when they meet a certain social or economic criteria?

Do you live in a false paradigm of cliques and exclusivity to the detriment of knowing and loving all the people God intends for you?

FORGIVE

Have you been excluded because someone has judged you according to the world's paradigm and not God's?

Forgive them that lack of insight. Lay the pain of that exclusion at the foot of the cross.

GIVE THANKS

Put aside what you think you know about acquiring power and position.

Instead, evaluate how well God has equipped you to walk humbly with Him, serving justice and loving mercy.

See the freedom there?

PRAY

Please, God, help me to strike arrogance from my heart.
Let me realign my life according to Your economy.
Let me treasure justice and mercy over power and prestige.
Let me remember that I am nothing without You,
and please put people in my path to
whom I can bring Your grace.

wednesday

MATTHEW 6:1-2

"Beware of practicing your piety before others
in order to be seen by them; for then you will
have no reward from your Father in heaven.
"So whenever you give alms, do not sound
a trumpet before you, as the hypocrites do
in the synagogues and in the streets, so that
they may be praised by others. Truly, I tell
you, they have received their reward."

FOR FURTHER CONTEMPLATION:

ROMANS 2:6-8

1 PETER 3:3-4

HEBREWS 11:6

Every family has one. If your family is large enough, you might have more than one: the child with the flair for the dramatic, the one who always demands center stage. We don't always recognize the pleading behind his eyes: Notice me, please. Assure me that I'm good enough for you to love me.

Or perhaps you know the attention seeker in the friend who is always telling you just how awful she is, hoping fervently that you will assure her that, of course, she's not.

Sometimes, the attention seeker is the person who burns up the phone lines, sowing seeds of discord while exchanging family gossip, playing one person against another in hopes of aligning all of them in favor of her, as if the family is divided into teams and she cannot possibly hold them all in her affection at once, nor can they all hold her.

For some people the need for attention is insatiable and the suggestion of quiet time alone or a thoughtful, extended period of listening is threatening, if not downright terrifying. They crave being at the center of the drama, often to the point of creating drama just so they have somewhere to be.

It's exhausting work, always questing after the spotlight, always focusing attention on oneself. It's a candle that often burns so fast and so straight down the center of the wick that it collapses in on itself in a heap of utter despair.

Attention seeking is pride amped up for all the world to see, even if not to recognize immediately. Its antidote, of course, is the cure-all: humility. Just as we don't always recognize attention seeking for what it is, we also can miss humility.

C. S. Lewis draws a very clear picture for us:

Do not imagine that if you meet a really humble man he will be what most people call 'humble' nowadays: he will not be a sort of greasy, smarmy person, who is always telling you that, of course, he is nobody. Probably all you will think about him is that he seemed a cheerful, intelligent chap who took a real interest in what you said to him. If you do dislike him it will be because you feel a little envious of anyone who seems to enjoy life so easily. He will not be thinking about humility: he will not be thinking about himself at all. (*Mere Christianity*)

"To enjoy life so easily" is exactly the opposite of what the attention seeker experiences. For her, life is a constant calling out, a constant reaching and striving to make everything about herself.

Lewis' quote, in its simplicity, points us to self-forgetfulness. The humble soul isn't overwrought with one-upping the person next to her to be sure that she isn't forgotten. The humble person forgets herself on purpose, focusing with concern on other people, intentionally fixing her gaze on God.

Attention seekers are people pleasers. Humble people devote their full time and attention to pleasing God. God doesn't need us to achieve in the spotlight. At the same time, God doesn't want us to beat ourselves up and dwell on our sins and the relative worthlessness they confer.

Instead, God wants us to know His love deep in our being and to extend that gracious good love to everyone in our sphere of influence.

This Lent, we look to the cross. God gave us the ultimate act of humility, the most stunning example of self-sacrifice. He bore our shame so that we could forget about ourselves and enjoy Him now—here in this real world that is so full of threats to our worth—and forever, in eternity, where we'll all relax into the reality of His abundant love.

ELIZABETH FOSS

HE WILL NOT BE THINKING ABOUT HUMILITY:
HE WILL NOT BE THINKING
ABOUT HIMSELF AT ALL.

MERE CHRISTIANITY

LECTIO DIVINA

LECTIO

Matthew 6:1-2
Today's verses are another excerpt from the Sermon on the Mount. Jesus doesn't say that piety, almsgiving, and fasting are bad, but that they must be done with the right spirit. Are we performing them for public esteem, or to please God and cultivate deeper holiness in our lives?

MEDITATIO

What personal message does the text have for me?

ORATIO

What do I say to the Lord in response to His word?

CONTEMPLATIO

What conversion of mind, heart, and life is He asking of me today?

How did I progress in living the Word today?

ACTIO

How will I make my life a gift for others in charity?
What does God want me to do today?

REPENT

Do you demand attention, always seeking the spotlight?

Do you thrive on drama, so you create it in order to sustain the attention of those around you?

Do you recount your faults to others in order to have them reassure you that you are good?

Do you fail to notice the need around you because you are so focused on yourself?

FORGIVE

Does someone demand center stage in your life and push you to the side in the process?

Forgive that sin and bring his need to be assured of his worth to the foot of the cross.

GIVE THANKS

Is there someone in your life who is always ready to drop what she's doing to meet your real needs?

Is there someone in your life who cheerfully listens while you pour out your heart?

PRAY

*Dear Jesus, make my life like Yours.
Help me to take my eyes off myself and
to see other people clearly.
Make me into the cheerful person
who is interested in others and
who enjoys life easily.*

(And God, please do this also for the attention seeker in my life.)

thursday

Do nothing from selfish ambition or conceit,
but in humility regard others as better than
yourselves. Let each of you look not to your
own interests, but to the interests of others.
Let the same mind be in you that was in
Christ Jesus,

who, though he was in the form of God,
   did not regard equality with God
   as something to be exploited,

but emptied himself,
   taking the form of a slave,
   being born in human likeness.
And being found in human form,

   he humbled himself
   and became obedient to the point of
death—
   even death on a cross.

FOR FURTHER CONTEMPLATION:

---

1 THESSALONIANS 5:14-15

ROMANS 12:16

I used to think I didn't have a pride problem. I know, I know. The first sign that someone probably has issues with pridefulness is her belief that she doesn't. But truth is, self-flagellation, more than self-promotion, always came more easily to me.

Once during spiritual direction, I expressed similar sentiments. "You suffer from a bad case of false humility," my wise spiritual director informed me. "Pride and vanity are tightly braided together, and you are grappling with both."

Huh? Little, lowly me? Vain, maybe, but prideful?

Throughout my life, I've tirelessly tried to put my best (read: perfect) self forward. As a teenager and young woman, I was so preoccupied with my outward beauty and using the scale as a barometer of my self-worth that I fell prey to anorexia and then bulimia. Even as I became rifle-thin, my cheeks would burn with humiliation when I remembered vicious middle school boys oinking at my chubbier self.

As a writer, I've sometimes longed for bigger bylines, or obsessed over an editing error in a final copy.

As a young mother, I so desperately wanted to be the perfect parent that I subscribed to magnanimous parenting principles and couldn't let go of them even when it was clear they weren't working for my children or my family.

Then, whenever I couldn't live up to any perfect ideal – and I never could—it was dangerously easy to fall into the trap of false humility. Oh, I am such a miserable sinner. I'm unworthy—a weak, good-for-nothing nobody.

So then what did I do? I tried harder, often to the point of burnout, anxiety, and abject misery.

But why? Because I was afraid. Of failure. Of unpopularity and rejection. Of losing control. Of people seeing the skeletons, dust bunnies, and mismatched shoes hiding in the closet.

Some of us may wrestle with more traditional pride, but we're equally fearful. Maybe we see others as not being worth our time and attention. That makes us no better than the playground bully who targets anyone on the social margins, putting others down to make us feel better about ourselves.

That's where the devil is hiding: in your belief that you or perhaps others are unworthy—even of God's mercy and love. The devil doesn't want you to move forward and serve others. He wants you stuck in your haughtiness or self-loathing.

But our Heavenly Father desires something different for you. He wants you to step forward in faith and introduce the world to your brave, authentic self, and to do everything out of love, not out of conceit.

Lent is a beautiful time to take stock of all the things God has done for you in your life and own it. That's not prideful. That's an act of gratitude.

None of us is really worthy of God's unending love and mercy. None of us deserved the gift of God sacrificing His only Son and His suffering of a brutal death just to redeem this broken, messy lot of us. We are all the weak, lowly, and fainthearted. The cross is the great equalizer. Jesus died for all of us—the haughty, the lowly, the very ones we judge, covet, compete with, or try to impress with our shiny, perfect veneers.

Jesus showed us how to be truly humble to the point of death.

Don't undermine His sacrifice. He's telling all of us as He hangs from the cross, arms outstretched, that we are worth it. With every last drop of blood, He lovingly whispers: You are worth it.

KATE WICKER

HE LOVINGLY WHISPERS: *YOU ARE WORTH IT.*

LECTIO DIVINA

LECTIO

Philippians 2:3-8
Paul's letter to the Philippians is his most deeply personal letter, and the writing in today's passage has been called the most beautiful in all his writings. It is a deep theological reflection on Christ's life, and displays Him as the model for Christian living.

MEDITATIO

What personal message does the text have for me?

ORATIO

What do I say to the Lord in response to His word?

CONTEMPLATIO

What conversion of mind, heart, and life is He asking of me today?

How did I progress in living the Word today?

ACTIO

How will I make my life a gift for others in charity?
What does God want me to do today?

REPENT

Do you judge yourself according to the false standards of this fallen world, striving for status or wealth or fame or outward beauty?

Do you dismiss other people as beneath you, not worth your time or attention or friendship, because you think that you are exalted above them?

FORGIVE

Has someone shamed you, caused your cheeks to burn with humiliation?

Forgive that now, and leave that memory at the foot of the cross.

GIVE THANKS

Do you recognize that God sees you as you are and He loves you more than anyone in this world ever could?

Do you know that your soul is beautiful, created in the image of the abundant, generous, glorious God and that He waits to clean out the muck and shine it for you so that the person you truly are—the soul that lives within—will shine forth into this temporary world?

PRAY

I'm a mess, God.
I get it all upside down and backwards.
I care about things that are fleeting and unimportant.
I build them up to be bigger than life, bigger than You.
And in doing so, I've missed people along the way,
people who seem inconsequential,
but who are really the work You intend for me.
Let me love them, Jesus.
Let me be truly humble and see
that they are what is of enduring value to You.
Let me bend low and lift the crosses
of the people in my path with my own roughened hands
instead of dismissing them with
a wave of manicured "perfection."

friday

GALATIANS 5:16-23

Live by the Spirit, I say, and do not gratify the desires of the flesh. For what the flesh desires is opposed to the Spirit, and what the Spirit desires is opposed to the flesh; for these are opposed to each other, to prevent you from doing what you want. But if you are led by the Spirit, you are not subject to the law. Now the works of the flesh are obvious: fornication, impurity, licentiousness, idolatry, sorcery, enmities, strife, jealousy, anger, quarrels, dissension, factions, envy, drunkenness, carousing, and things like these. I am warning you, as I warned you before: those who do such things shall not inherit the kingdom of God. By contrast, the fruit of the Spirit is love, joy, peace, patience, kindness, generosity, faithfulness, gentleness, and self-control. There is no law against such things.

FOR FURTHER CONTEMPLATION:

ISAIAH 58:3-7

PHILIPPIANS 4:10-13

ALL OF PSALM 90

Fasting is such a gift. In the back of nearly every woman's mind is the idea that she can give up XYZ foods for Lent and find herself a dress size smaller at Easter. Pride tells us we can do this fasting thing, and what's more, we'll be better looking for our efforts. We are loath to admit it, but we confuse the Lenten fast for a weight loss diet sanctioned and blessed by the Church.

When I say fasting is a gift, I don't mean it's the foolproof gimmick that yields a slimmer you in just six weeks. Fasting is a gift because it peels back the layers of pride and gluttony and, hopefully, yields a humbler you by Easter.

The glutton overindulges. Most commonly, when we think of gluttony, we think of food, and surely, there are those among us who eat too much. There are also those among us who drink too much or spend too much or work too much or watch too much Netflix. All those binges are occasions of gluttony. They are filling our holes with something, searching for the thing which will make us content at last.

But we are never content. We are only bloated to uncomfortable tightness with things.

There are no fruits of the Spirit, no love, joy, peace, patience, kindness, generosity, faithfulness, gentleness, and self-control. There is only the empty feeling of wanting more story when we get to the end of Season Seven, and the crumbs and salt in the bottom of the kettle-fried potato chip bag. We've binged on something other than God.

Fasting tells us we don't need Netflix or chips. Further, fasting can tell us we don't really need meat, or warm water for a shower, or those five minutes after the snooze alarm, or coffee.

When we give up things that are extra, it heightens our awareness of greed, of wastefulness. But when we give up things that most people would agree are legitimate needs—if only for a short time—it heightens our humility. We begin to understand that we really, truly, bottom line have one honest-to-goodness-need.

We need Christ.

We are nothing apart from God.

God doesn't need us to give up meat on Friday. God doesn't even need us to "do something extra." We need Him. We need to know that we are utterly dependent on Him and that the people we do life with are dependent on us to be His hands and feet and voice here on earth. He works through us, but only if we let Him, only if we are so tuned in to our dependence on Him that we empty ourselves of our agenda and let Him pour Himself in.

Fasting makes us hungry. Holy fasting makes us hungry for God—for His plan and His perfect provision, the plan and the provision that yield perfect peace.

ELIZABETH FOSS

FASTING IS A GIFT BECAUSE IT PEELS BACK THE LAYERS OF PRIDE AND GLUTTONY AND, HOPEFULLY, YIELDS A HUMBLER YOU BY EASTER.

LECTIO DIVINA

LECTIO

Galatians 5:16-23
One of the main themes of Galatians is the ministry of the Holy Spirit in relation to the Christian life. Here, Paul discusses the internal war between the desires of the flesh—our fallen nature—and the Holy Spirit's calling.

MEDITATIO

What personal message does the text have for me?

ORATIO

What do I say to the Lord in response to His word?

CONTEMPLATIO

What conversion of mind, heart, and life is He asking of me today?

How did I progress in living the Word today?

ACTIO

How will I make my life a gift for others in charity?
What does God want me to do today?

REPENT

Do you have a right spirit about fasting? Do you wear sackcloth and ashes and moan and complain or do you embrace sacrifice as a way to become more Christlike?

Are you attached to things of this world and do you make idols of them, prioritizing your life so that you don't have to be without them?

Do you recognize your complete need for Christ and the way that you can be content in Him, regardless of the creature comforts in your surroundings?

FORGIVE

Is there someone whose influence has invited you into gluttony—whether of food and drink or of another kind of binging? Forgive them, and pray that they recognize the God-sized hole and fill it with Him.

GIVE THANKS

A day at a time, a moment at a time, we keep a Lenten fast. Give thanks for the times today that He gave you the grace to fast from the world and lean hard into His strength.

PRAY

Oh, Lord, make me humble.
Help me to fast well.
Teach me that the one thing I need is You.
Show me how to be Your hands and feet,
how to speak Your truth into the lives
of the people You send my way.
Let me seek to give to Your children
much more than I seek my own comfort.
Let me see that You are the one true Comforter.

saturday

MATTHEW 6:19-21

"Do not store up for yourselves treasures on earth, where moth and rust consume and where thieves break in and steal; but store up for yourselves treasures in heaven, where neither moth nor rust consumes and where thieves do not break in and steal. For where your treasure is, there will your heart be also."

FOR FURTHER CONTEMPLATION:

ROMANS 12:13

1 PETER 4:7-9

MATTHEW 10:40

EPHESIANS 9:28

2 CORINTHIANS 9:7

ACTS 4:34-35

HEBREWS 13:5

MATTHEW 6:25-30

When I think of greed, my first thought is the cartoon miser, living miserably alone while money piles up around him. (See what I did there? Misers are miserable.) Greed is bigger than the character, though. It's the insatiable desire to acquire. It is discontent that lies and entices us to believe that we don't have enough. Very few of us look at the bottom line of our household budgets and decide that we've got plenty to live on, so we'll give the rest away. Instead, we keep expanding our way of life and adding to our coffers, even if just to tuck away for unforeseen needs later or to plan prudentially for retirement. We seem to habitually stress over our perceived "lack" and somewhere we cross the fine line between prudent stewardship and sinful greed.

Jesus had quite a lot to say about money, possessions, and greed. Here, living in a place of great prosperity, we need all the help we can get to align our thinking with the Gospel. Jesus told us that we will perish if we store our treasures anywhere but in heaven. But what does that mean, practically speaking, and how can we guard against sin?

How we handle our money tells us a great deal about how much we trust Providence. Will God give us what we need or not? Do we treasure Christ or do we worship at the altar of acquisition? Acquiring wealth is not a sin. People who have sums of money and know that money is a gift to steward for the Kingdom just like any other gift can advance the Gospel in extraordinary ways. Saint Paul addressed the Romans with a very simple tool to be used by people who have plenty: contribute to the needs of the saints and seek to show hospitality.

For us, in a modern land of plenty, the marching orders are clear. Where there is need, we meet the need. Then, we actively seek ways to show hospitality—to open our very comfortable homes and shelter and feed and clothe and comfort. We don't just write a check (though checks are good and people depend on those checks), but look for ways to draw people into our lives so we can love them there. That's hospitality. That's an antidote to greed.

There is freedom in offering hospitality with warm hearts and open doors. This is not about entertaining or about fancy guest soaps. It's about throwing a cloak of love over someone who doesn't have one. God will give us what we need to do that. We know that God is generous. He gave us His only Son so that with every new day we can expect new mercy. That's over-the-top generosity. When we look at giving, we start with His example, which is also His promise. He will be there for us. We can't outgive God. So we can give with courage. "He who did not withhold his own Son, but gave him up for all of us, will he not with him also give us everything else?" (Romans 8:32)

When we open our homes and our hearts to give generously, we unite ourselves with a generous God. If we remain tight-fisted and we stack those bags of gold like the miser does, it's because we are afraid. Fear is the jailer who will make us miserable. God will supply all our needs according to his riches in glory in Christ Jesus. (Philippians 4:19) That sentence is rich in and of itself. Claim it and seek ways to be hospitable. I promise you'll find them.

ELIZABETH FOSS

IT'S ABOUT THROWING A CLOAK OF LOVE OVER SOMEONE WHO DOESN'T HAVE ONE. GOD WILL GIVE US WHAT WE NEED TO DO THAT.

LECTIO DIVINA

LECTIO

Matthew 6:19-21
Jesus warns his listeners that they must set their minds on heavenly things instead of earthly things. This is a continuation of the deeper call to personal holiness that Matthew has been stressing throughout his Gospel, and especially in the Sermon on the Mount.

MEDITATIO

What personal message does the text have for me?

ORATIO

What do I say to the Lord in response to His word?

CONTEMPLATIO

What conversion of mind, heart, and life is He asking of me today?

How did I progress in living the Word today?

ACTIO

How will I make my life a gift for others in charity?
What does God want me to do today?

REPENT

Do you miss the point that all that you have belongs to God for the purpose of extending His love, and so you are miserly with your possessions?

Do you hold back in meeting a need because you're afraid you won't have enough left for yourself?

Do you withhold hospitality because you think you have to "entertain" in a perfect household?

Do you hesitate to invite someone in when you could provide food or shelter or comfort or companionship?

FORGIVE

Have you been turned away hungry or cold or lonely?

Forgive that hardness of heart and bury yourself in His tender heart.

GIVE THANKS

Has someone offered you hospitality and met your needs?

PRAY

Dear Lord,
let me trust You with all
You've given me.
Open my eyes to the needs around me
and inspire me to open my heart
to give with Your generosity.

third week of lent

EVERY DAY THIS WEEK:

SCRIPTURE READINGS

ESSAY REFLECTION

LECTIO DIVINA

REPENT, FORGIVE, GIVE THANKS

PRAYER

MORE THIS WEEK:

WEEKLY SCRIPTURE MEMORY

WEEKLY SCRIPTURE MEMORY

THIRD SUNDAY OF LENT

———————————

Here, we continue to memorize Colossians 3:12-17.

Over the course of Lent, we will commit to memory the entire passage Paul gives to the Colossians in order to tell them how to live a new life in the Lord. Taking it just a little bit at a time and building week after week, we can commit the passage to memory and—even better—we can hide it in our hearts.

———————————

COLOSSIANS 3:14

ABOVE ALL, CLOTHE YOURSELVES WITH LOVE,
WHICH BINDS EVERYTHING TOGETHER
IN PERFECT HARMONY.

sunday

Taken together, these passages from Colossians and Ephesians emphasize charity (love) as both the motivation and the foundation of all other virtues. We carefully consider vices that were observed in the people of Colassae and Ephesus (and are clearly observable in our day as well). Calling out one sin at a time, Saint Paul explains how love triumphs over them and yields virtue instead.

Today, read through each of these verses carefully, noting how they work together. What is the overall message they hold? Over the next week, we'll pull out smaller passages within these verses to consider one at a time.

COLOSSIANS 3:1-17

COLOSSIANS 3:23-25

EPHESIANS 1:15-23

EPHESIANS 4:17-32

EPHESIANS 5:1-2

THIRD WEEK OF LENT

For the next week, we'll sit with parts of Saint Paul's letters to the Colossians and to the Ephesians, looking carefully at the repeated words in these messages and considering them in the light of the idea that the Holy Spirit thought them so important, He reiterated Himself.

It's important to read these verses in context first, to understand how Saint Paul urges us to throw off the old ways, not because he's making our lives difficult, but because he wants to encourage us. If we let go of the old—if we put the sin of Adam and Eve to death—we can lean with our whole hearts into Christ and the new creation He wants to make of us.

It is generally accepted by most scholars that Saint Paul wrote to both the Colossians and the Ephesians from prison in Rome. Paul had never met the new believers in Colossae. They'd converted under the teaching of Epaphras and it was Epaphras who told Saint Paul about them. He addresses them as saints—fellow believers who will inherit the Kingdom—and he wants to encourage them and strengthen their moral resolve. The Holy Spirit uses Saint Paul's words to encourage us, too.

In the beginning of the epistle to the Ephesians, Saint Paul reminds the believers that the mysteries of Christian life on earth and after death require divine assistance to be understood. He exhorts them to pray for that grace.

I pray that the God of our Lord Jesus Christ, the Father of glory, may give you a spirit of wisdom and revelation as you come to know him, so that, with the eyes of your heart enlightened, you may know what is the hope to which he has called you, what are the riches of his glorious inheritance among the saints, and what is the immeasurable greatness of his power for us who believe, according to the working of his great power. (Ephesians 1:17-19)

That seems a good place for us to begin, as well.

In the next week, Saint Paul will tell us that ours can be an entirely new nature, one of virtue and its joy. He invites us—no, exhorts us—to shrug off the old, ill-fitting, utterly constraining ways and to put on love. The cloak of love can transform us if we let it. Today, let's look at the messages and ask the Holy Spirit to show us a clear picture of the new creation He desires us to be.

ELIZABETH FOSS

LECTIO DIVINA

LECTIO

Taken together, these passages from Colossians and Ephesians emphasize charity (love) as both the motivation and the foundation of all other virtues. We carefully consider vices that were observed in the people of Colassae and Ephesus (and are clearly observable in our day as well). Calling out one sin at a time, Saint Paul explains how love triumphs over them and yields virtue instead.

MEDITATIO

What personal message does the text have for me?

ORATIO

What do I say to the Lord in response to His word?

CONTEMPLATIO

What conversion of mind, heart, and life is He asking of me today?

How did I progress in living the Word today?

Third Sunday of Lent
REFLECTION

What is the hope to which God has called you?
How does it stand in contrast with the clarion
call of your everyday world?

GIVE THANKS

God has chosen you (Ephesians
1:3-6) for life with Him.

He will save you according to
His love and mercy.

Thank Him for that. Just start
there.

PRAY

For this reason I bow my knees before the Father,
from whom every family in heaven and on earth is named, that
according to the riches of his glory he may grant me
to be strengthened with might through his Spirit in the inner man,
and that Christ may dwell in my hearts through faith;
that I, being rooted and grounded in love, may have power to
comprehend with all the saints what is the breadth and length and
height and depth, and to know the love of Christ which surpasses
knowledge, that I may be filled with all the fullness of God. Now
to him who by the power at work within us is able to do far more
abundantly than all that we ask or think, to him be glory in the
church and in Christ Jesus to all generations, for ever and ever.

Amen.

(Adapted from St. Paul's Prayer for the readers in Ephesus.
Ephesians 3:14-21)

ABOVE ALL | THIRD WEEK OF LENT

monday

COLOSSIANS 3:5-6

Put to death, therefore, whatever in you is
earthly: fornication, impurity, passion, evil
desire, and greed (which is idolatry). On
account of these the wrath of God is coming
on those who are disobedient. These are the
ways you also once followed, when you were
living that life.

FOR FURTHER CONTEMPLATION:

COLOSSIANS 3:18

EPHESIANS 5:21-33

EPHESIANS 4:22-23

PHILIPPIANS 4:8-9

ROMANS 12:1-2

PHILIPPIANS 4:8-9

Put to death, therefore, whatever in you is earthly... (Colossians 3:5)

Saint Paul is very clear on selfishness in his letter to the Colossians, yet it's in our concupiscent nature to consider and act primarily upon our own needs and desires. We're often encouraged to put ourselves first, to make sure we are satisfied in every situation.

His first phrase, "put to death," brings to mind the death of Christ, the central death in the Bible. It also reminds us of another death, however: that which was caused by our first parents' sinfulness. These deaths were complementary events, the first necessitating the second—both tragic, but with far different motives and outcomes.

When Adam and Eve ate the fruit of the tree of knowledge, their greed earned us death. When Christ, through His perfect self-sacrifice, chose to die for us, He earned us all eternal life. Two deaths: one was self-serving and brought sinfulness and pain, while the other was wholly giving and redeemed the entire human race.

...fornication, impurity, passion, evil desire, and greed (which is idolatry). (Colossians 3:5)

Our sexuality longs to mirror the type of life-giving love that Christ models, and yet time and again, we recreate the sins of Adam and Eve. We think of ourselves and our pleasure alone. Saint Pope John Paul II, a great theologian on human love, aptly describes the heart as a battlefield, when he says, "The heart has become a battlefield between love and lust. The more lust dominates the heart, the less the heart experiences the nuptial meaning of the body." (John Paul II, General Audience, July 23, 1980). In our humanity, we struggle between the desire to be in true, sacrificial communion with another, as Christ is with His Church, and the earthly pleasure of our own physical fulfillment. It's a battle that occurs within each of us in unique ways.

Sexual sin takes the most intimate of encounters and perverts it into hollow objectification. It clouds our sensibilities, blinds us to true beauty, and deafens us to the truth found in the word of God. When sex is entirely life-giving, it not only carries the possibility of creating new life, but also nourishes the life of our spouse and our love for them. Anything we do in humility and loving service for our spouse (or future spouse) will nourish us as well.

On account of these the wrath of God is coming on those who are disobedient. These are the ways you also once followed, when you were living that life. (Colossians 5:6)

Any "earthly" desire which we distort into an idol—sex, alcohol, tobacco, monetary wealth—can displace and distort the love set upon our hearts by our Creator. The irony is that each idol is a misguided attempt to find fulfillment, yet we seek it in something other than the complete love of Jesus Christ. None of these will satiate us, nor bring us complete happiness, because only through Christ have we been made new. We are no longer meant for the earthly flesh, but for eternal life with a God who wants our entire beings to be united with Him.

As Saint Paul says, "fornication, immorality, passion, evil desire, and greed" will bring upon us the wrath of God. Not because He doesn't want us to be pleased, but precisely because He has a perfect plan for our union with Him. All attempts to subvert His will lead us away from Him. Yet whenever we "put to death" the earthly desires and cloak ourselves with the true beauty bestowed upon us by God, we draw nearer to Him.

MICAELA DARR

THE HEART HAS BECOME A BATTLEFIELD
BETWEEN LOVE AND LUST.
THE MORE LUST DOMINATES THE HEART,
THE LESS THE HEART EXPERIENCES
THE NUPTIAL MEANING OF THE BODY."

JOHN PAUL II, GENERAL AUDIENCE
JULY 23, 1980

LECTIO DIVINA

LECTIO

Colossians 3:5-6
Throughout his letter to the Colossians, Paul urges the readers to conform their lives to Christ. Today, Paul offers concrete examples of how to do that—by putting aside impurity, immorality, and other vices. This message is restated throughout the Pauline epistles, especially in the Letter to the Ephesians, as seen in today's second verse.

MEDITATIO

What personal message does the text have for me?

ORATIO

What do I say to the Lord in response to His word?

CONTEMPLATIO

What conversion of mind, heart, and life is He asking of me today?

How did I progress in living the Word today?

ACTIO

How will I make my life a gift for others in charity?

What does God want me to do today?

R E P E N T

Is your love life-giving, or are you selfish?

F O R G I V E

Has someone offended you by sexually defiling the image of our Lord that lives in you?

Deep breath. Forgive that painful sin and shed the heavy garment of despair that comes with it.

Take comfort in the arms of the Father.

G I V E   T H A N K S

Have you been blessed with someone who has respected your sexuality and honored you as an image of God?

That's a beautiful blessing. Give thanks!

PRAY

Dear Lord,
Thank you for the beautiful,
life-giving gift of human love.
Help me to be a good and
grateful steward of its power.

tuesday

COLOSSIANS 3:8

But now you must get rid of all such things—anger, wrath, malice, slander, and abusive language from your mouth.

FOR FURTHER CONTEMPLATION:

EPHESIANS 4:26-27

B
e angry, but do not sin. There are over 365 Biblical references to God's anger. One for every day of the year. Clearly, anger itself is not a sin. There is such a thing as righteous anger. Saint Paul tells the Ephesians that they can be angry as long as they don't sin in anger.

Go ahead; try that. I'll wait.

It's exceedingly difficult to be angry without sinning. The fine line is very fine indeed. The anger we feel bubbling to explosiveness is usually rooted in fear. Something threatens us and that makes us angry. The anger isn't a sin; it's actually the energy we need to make things right. But the manifestation of that anger is what usually gets us into trouble. When we take an honest look at our anger (which is also difficult to do in the heat of anger), we find that often there's some selfishness mixed into our response. We are angry because we want what we want when we want it, and then we don't get it. We want respect or obedience or order or efficiency, or any number of things that we hold important. And it infuriates us (and threatens us) to be denied. So we get mad. Ours is rarely a truly, purely righteous anger. What to do then, with this sinful anger?

Saint Paul's advice is super simple. "Put it all aside."

Just do it.

All of it. Put it aside. Even if all you ever knew as a child were outbursts of angry temper. Even if you've had a tendency to throw formidable tantrums since you were a toddler. Even if you think you have every right to let your blood boil over onto everyone around you. Put it all aside.

You are new creation in Christ. He died to take away the sin of your anger. You were baptized in the Holy Spirit so that He would live in you and help you manage your anger. When was the last time you tapped into that resource? An angry outburst is a desire of your flesh, pure and simple. It's the evil one, inspiring your behavior. The good news? There's a solution to the problem of anger.

"Live by the Spirit, I say, and do not gratify the desires of the flesh." (Galatians 5:16)

Confess anger as a sin and in the moment ask the Holy Spirit to help you to control it. Yes, you can. You've controlled anger in the past. That time you stood in a grocery store, blood boiling, but you didn't yell at your kids because you didn't want people to stare? The time you were absolutely furious at the staff who works for you, but you didn't lose it in front of the client, both because you didn't want to lose the client and you didn't want anyone to call HR? You can control your anger.

Think about how much better you can control it with God on your side.

Jesus was angry. He gave us examples of His own anger so that we could understand that it is possible to be angry without sinning. He overturned tables without sinning. What did He not do? He did not sin against the dignity of another person. He did not treat them with contempt.

He sort of had a superpower in the moments of His anger, though. Jesus had the advantage of being able to see into people's hearts and to know exactly the right tone to strike when the energy of His anger compelled Him to take action.

Therein lies our path towards sinless anger.

When you are angry, even when you are assured in your own heart that your anger is righteous, look into the heart of the person who is the object of your anger. Ask the angry Spirit of the Jesus in the temple to be with you in that moment.

Every single time.

Ask Him: What is in the heart of this person who has so angered me at this moment? Help me, Jesus, to see his heart, to know how best to react and to respond with kindness even in my anger. Please show me, too, Lord, exactly what threatens me in this moment. What do I fear I have lost here? Let me see clearly both my heart and his and help me to use my anger for good, reconciling us both to one another and to You.

Put that sinful anger aside. Put it all aside. Put on love.

ELIZABETH FOSS

LECTIO DIVINA

LECTIO

Colossians 3:8
The major theme of Colossians is that fullness of life is available to all, but only through life in Christ. To find that life, Paul tells the Colossians—and us— to put aside our sins, especially those that occur from angry and malicious speech.

MEDITATIO

What personal message does the text have for me?

ORATIO

What do I say to the Lord in response to His word?

CONTEMPLATIO

What conversion of mind, heart, and life is He asking of me today?

How did I progress in living the Word today?

ACTIO

How will I make my life a gift for others in charity?
What does God want me to do today?

REPENT

In your anger, have you lost your temper?

In your anger, have you sinned against the dignity of another person?

FORGIVE

Has someone lashed out at you in anger and bruised your spirit?

Forgive the sin of temper and rashness.

Let yourself be comforted by the gentle Jesus who hangs on the cross to forgive even the furious.

GIVE THANKS

We can make amends for the times we've sinned in anger. It's never too late for an apology to be effective.

Resolve to apologize for an angry outburst.

List the ways you are thankful for second chances and for grace.

PRAY

O Lord, you have searched me and known me.
You know when I sit down and when I rise up;
you discern my thoughts from far away...
Even before a word is on my tongue, O Lord,
you know it completely. (Psalm 139)
Please be with me in my moments of anger.
Infuse me with Your Spirit and help me to see the hearts
of the people I encounter.
Let me walk in Your peace, God.

wednesday

EPHESIANS 4:29

Let no evil talk come out of your mouths, but
only what is useful for building up, as there
is need, so that your words may give grace to
those who hear.

FOR FURTHER CONTEMPLATION:

JAMES 3:1-9

COLOSSIANS 3:7-8

MATTHEW 12:36-37

Oh, the sins we commit when we open our mouths to speak! While we are often careless, even reckless, with the things we say, God is not. Jesus warns us about our careless words.

How often do we really speak as if we will have to account for every word we utter? Every single word matters and the tempter delights in the smorgasbord of tools at his disposal to entice you to sin against your co-worker, your housemate, your child, even your spouse.

We can damage another person with our words when they are present or behind their backs. When we revile someone else, they are there to hear it. Maybe it's in jest or maybe it's a passive-aggressive stab, but we drive a stake into someone's heart when we spotlight someone else's faults for everyone to see, even if we're "just teasing." Those words embarrass and undercut a relationship.

Be careful with that joke. Derision is a sin. When we make fun of someone else's shortcomings or mannerisms at his or her expense, even behind someone's back, we have wandered into dangerous territory. Ripping the image of God is rarely the lighthearted jaunt we think it is. We damage someone else's reputation at our own expense. Not only does making someone else the butt of (poor) jokes make us look foolish to our audience, it injures the body of Christ.

Often, we fall prey to the temptation to wound someone else when they are not present. Usually in an attempt to build ourselves up, we tear someone else down. We either want to look better than the object of our calumny (uttering a falsehood about someone) or detraction (telling something that is true but that harms a reputation), or we want to elevate our status by sharing news no one else has yet heard. We sin at the expense of someone else. We have told a tale that momentarily makes us feel powerful, but ultimately erodes our own souls and hurts the person about whom we told it.

In the life of a family or a community, it is sometimes necessary to have conversations about people. Those conversations should be thoughtful and careful, never reckless. When the need arises to discuss someone else's faults, every word should be matched with equal words of prayer.

Parents, be especially careful when you speak about your children. We teach our children to gossip when we talk to them about other people, especially when we talk with one sibling about another in unnecessary, unkind ways. While every family will have the need to share information with one another, guard your tongues! Discussing the faults and poor behavior of one member of a community with another member sets a pattern for tearing down relationships. Mocking or deriding people in their absence nurtures a sense of distrust among those present. Parents are charged to be especially careful to protect the integrity of a family by being reserved and careful when they speak. Such care requires tremendous effort and not a little prudence, but the tentacles of the sins of the tongue are far-reaching and tenacious. Better not to let them grow in the first place.

There are times when we need advice or encouragement and we need a safe place to vent about true struggles with someone else. God knows that. And really, usually, we know, too, if our words are ultimately constructive. For all those other times—and there are many—frequent confession and a sincere desire to replace poor habits of the tongue with more prudent ones are necessities for our spiritual health.

ELIZABETH FOSS

LECTIO DIVINA

LECTIO

Ephesians 4:29
Paul restates his exhortation to put aside evil speech in his letter to the Ephesians, with an addition: we should only speak things that are "useful for building up" so that our words may give grace. Speech that is careless, untruthful, and slanderous threatens the unity of the Body of Christ.

MEDITATIO

What personal message does the text have for me?

ORATIO

What do I say to the Lord in response to His word?

CONTEMPLATIO

What conversion of mind, heart, and life is He asking of me today?

How did I progress in living the Word today?

ACTIO

How will I make my life a gift for others in charity?
What does God want me to do today?

REPENT

Have you gossiped? Have you made other people the butt of your jokes? Have you spoken untruths or spread stories about others?

Have you spoken ill of one member of your family or community to another?

FORGIVE

Has someone wounded you with words?

Forgive transgressions of the tongue and leave the pain caused by someone else's unkind words at the foot of Jesus who speaks the truth in love.

GIVE THANKS

Did someone speak words of gracious kindness to you today?

Did you share words of encouragement with someone else?

Did you hold your tongue and take your critical or derisive thoughts to God instead of speaking them aloud?

PRAY

Sweet Jesus,
let the words that come from my mouth
be always inspired by Your word.
Let me know so well the way that You
speak to me that I pick up Your cadence
and Your accent and most of all, Your integrity.
Let my speech be such a reflection
of Your Scripture that listeners will have
trouble distinguishing where
You end and I begin.

ABOVE ALL | THIRD WEEK OF LENT

thursday

COLOSSIANS 3:9-10

Do not lie to one another, seeing that you have stripped off the old self with its practices and have clothed yourselves with the new self, which is being renewed in knowledge according to the image of its creator.

FOR FURTHER CONTEMPLATION:

ZECHARIAH 8:16

EPHESIANS 4:29-32

EPHESIANS 4:25

Our words have such power. We can discourage and tear down and suck the very life out of someone with the choices we make for our voices.

The Lord despises poor verbal choices. (Proverbs 6:16-17)

He wants us to encourage one another and build each other up, not just some times, but all times. (1 Thessalonians 5:11) Lies—even little lies—tear away at the fabric of community, whether that community is a family or a sorority or a parish. A thread at a time, each untruth is a sin against one another until the tapestry of love and trust is shot through with holes.

If we lie enough, we begin to deceive ourselves, losing track of who we really are.

Saint Paul pulls no punches: stop lying. He tells us to choose God, to choose love, to choose truth—all the time. And that's the thing about lying: it so easily becomes a habit. We tell a little lie, usually to save face (pride) or to avoid offense or conflict, and then that little lie grows, or we tell another little lie and then another, until it's just so easy to lie, and we forget altogether that we are people of truth.

We have to commit to throwing off the dirty rags of little lies, lest their stench stink up the truth we want to live. For Christians, our community is one body in Christ. We belong to one another; we are all members of His body. Lying disrupts the communion between body parts. It makes it so the body isn't truly communicating with itself.

It's hard to tell the truth about oneself. Lying is rooted in fear; we are afraid of what will happen in the light of truth. Ultimately though, what happens in truth is harmony. When we are true to ourselves and true to others, we live in peace.

We are called to genuine kindness; it isn't for some of us, for the "soft" among us. It is for all of us. When we throw off the old life, we pull on the cloak of kindness. Lying is a sin against kindness. God wants better for us in our relationships. His kindness calls us to repentance and to His grace. When we take a chance and reject the temptation to lie and replace it instead with vulnerability and genuine kindness towards one another, we become vessels of grace. When we refuse to lie, we refuse to sin against honest communication. As Saint Augustine reminds us, this is a simple issue of treating others as we wish to be treated. He wrote, "I have had experience of many who wished to deceive, but not one who wished to be deceived." (*Confessions*, Book X, Chapter XXIII)

Lying ultimately destroys. It destroys our relationships with one another. It destroys our sense of self. And if it becomes a habit (as it so easily can), it eats away at our friendship with Christ. Finally, remember, "A false witness will not go unpunished, and a liar will not escape." (Proverbs 19:5)

It's time to tell the truth.

ELIZABETH FOSS

WE ARE CALLED TO GENUINE *KINDNESS*

LECTIO DIVINA

LECTIO

Colossians 3:9-10
Paul places an extraordinary emphasis on the importance of how we speak and what we say. In both Colossians and Ephesians, he warns against the cancer of angry and malicious speech. Today, he continues this theme, by telling the Colossians to stop lying. Lies tear down the body of Christ, of which we are all a part. Truth-telling and kindness build it up.

MEDITATIO

What personal message does the text have for me?

ORATIO

What do I say to the Lord in response to His word?

CONTEMPLATIO

What conversion of mind, heart, and life is He asking of me today?

How did I progress in living the Word today?

ACTIO

How will I make my life a gift for others in charity?
What does God want me to do today?

REPENT

Do you make a false witness of your life because you aren't honest and sincere about who you really are?

Do you lie, even just a little?

FORGIVE

Has someone lied to you?

Has someone lied about you?

Forgive every little lie and all the big lies.

Let them lie—at the foot of His cross.

GIVE THANKS

Who are the people you know who extend genuine kindness and words that build you up?

PRAY

*Dear, sweet Jesus,
please guard my mouth.
Let my words be sincere and
truthful and altogether honest.
Develop in me a sense of truth
and help me to cultivate it in everything
I do and say and write.*

ABOVE ALL | THIRD WEEK OF LENT

friday

SIRACH 11:10-14

My child, do not busy yourself with many
matters;
   if you multiply activities, you will not be
held blameless.
If you pursue, you will not overtake,
   and by fleeing you will not escape.

There are those who work and struggle and
hurry,
   but are so much the more in want.

There are others who are slow and need help,
   who lack strength and abound in poverty;
but the eyes of the Lord look kindly upon
them;
   he lifts them out of their lowly condition
and raises up their heads
   to the amazement of the many.

Good things and bad, life and death,
   poverty and wealth, come from the Lord.

FOR FURTHER CONTEMPLATION:

COLOSSIANS 3:23-25

EPHESIANS 4:28

THIRD WEEK OF LENT

Sloth, an age-old vice, has transformed itself into an even deadlier progressive version than its previous iteration. Few people I know identify with the sloth: an ugly animal, still and frequently sleeping in a tree, which has been known to be so loath to move that it would rather starve than inch towards the tree's leaves. I live in a high-powered, high-energy world where people are rarely still, never mind still enough to starve themselves.

Here in this world, we are both Crazy Busy and Lazy Busy. Crazy Busy is the over-scheduled, over-pressured existence of a society who centers their lives on being upwardly mobile. It's a sin of pride and over-achievement in the true sense of the word. It's an issue for another day.

Lazy Busy is the modern day manifestation of acedia, a spiritual listlessness that threatens to starve our souls. "*Acedia* is evenings without number obliterated by television, evenings neither of entertainment nor of education but of narcoticized defense against time and duty. Above all, acedia is apathy, the refusal to engage the pathos of other lives and of God's life with them." (Neuhaus, Freedom for Ministry, 227) It's escapism via activity.

Acedia is the exhausted defeat that comes with failing to rest in God and to stop long enough to listen to His desire for our activity. Work drives us unceasingly, but it doesn't truly fill us and sustain us because what we are doing isn't fully His will for

TRUTH IS ETERNAL.
TRUTH IS TRUTH,
NO MATTER HOW
SOCIETY PROGRESSES.

us; it's not exactly what He wants us to be doing. We are working for something other than God: power, prestige, more money than we truly need, affirmation. So, in our stupefied, overworked, and exhausted state, we retreat frequently into listless, mostly electronic, gray zones of least resistance.

We still appear busy, but we're emotionally numb. Our planners are well-inked, but we are moving from engagement to engagement, resenting the people who interrupt our business, annoyed by unplanned needs of people in our care, and, often, unwilling to adjust our overly-filled schedules to make room for genuine spiritual work. Instead, we crave this weird gray comfort, letting precious minutes (even hours) slip away to mindless scrolling on handheld devices that literally force us to look down, instead of into someone else's eyes. We arrive home at night so spent by the day, that the only energy we have left is what it takes to click the remote control and be carried into the mindless oblivion of yet another screen.

Sometimes we work ourselves into acedia, keeping ourselves busy in order to numb ourselves to the pathos of the lives around us. That is laziness because entering into the pathos of others' lives is hard work. Busyness avoids the hard work. Busyness allows each member of a family to occupy himself with a different screen at the table instead of putting forth the effort to talk. Busyness crams our weekends full of activities because a little white space for just being together is scary. Busyness is lazy when it means that you stay late at the office, just finishing a few more tasks, because you don't have the emotional energy for a difficult (or even friendly) conversation at home.

The acedia that is born of overworking for things God never intended is deadly; it breeds boredom with people who matter most, then boredom with God, then boredom with life itself. It's a slow spiritual suicide.

Jesus comes alongside you in your busyness if you let Him. He can help you discern what is honest work and what is really robbing you of the time and energy to do honest work. He'll show you how to have ample time for the souls entrusted to your care. He wants so much for you to be able to look into the eyes of the people you love and see recognition and affection there.

ELIZABETH FOSS

LECTIO DIVINA

LECTIO

Sirach 11:10-14

Sirach is one of the deuterocanonical books of the Bible—it's found in Catholic and Orthodox Bibles, but not Protestant ones. One of the Wisdom books, Sirach is a collection of sayings written between 200 and 175 B.C. The book offers guidance for all aspects of human existence and is focused on conduct in daily life and the proper management of personal affairs.

MEDITATIO

What personal message does the text have for me?

ORATIO

What do I say to the Lord in response to His word?

CONTEMPLATIO

What conversion of mind, heart, and life is He asking of me today?

How did I progress in living the Word today?

ACTIO

How will I make my life a gift for others in charity?
What does God want me to do today?

REPENT

Do you spend too much time in front of screens in search of something to fill your cravings, missing that what you really crave is God?

Do you spend too much time at your job because you don't want to face the work of your relationships?

Do you favor one of your children (or siblings or parents) over another with your time and attention because it's just easier and more rewarding?

FORGIVE

Has someone else's acedia slowly shut you out of a meaningful relationship?

Forgive the sin and know that the crucified Lord hears and sees you.

GIVE THANKS

Is someone happy to see you when you walk through the door at night?

Does a child seek your attention over and over again during the day?

Is there a friend who keeps calling despite the fact that you've just been too busy for her?

PRAY

Lord,
lead me gently, but firmly,
away from the things that numb me
to the other people in my life.
Help me to genuinely rest
instead of anesthetizing
my tired spirit
with busyness.

saturday

COLOSSIANS 3:16-17

Let the word of Christ dwell in you richly;
teach and admonish one another in all
wisdom; and with gratitude in your hearts
sing psalms, hymns, and spiritual songs to
God. And whatever you do, in word or deed,
do everything in the name of the Lord Jesus,
giving thanks to God the Father through him.

FOR FURTHER CONTEMPLATION:

1 THESSALONIANS 5:16-18

JOB 1

EPHESIANS 5:1-2

There's nothing quite like the highs and lows of marriage and family life to break a heart wide open and flip it inside out. Over the years, I've come to realize that this wrecking and rebuilding is necessary for my sanctification—a precious gift for which I should be on my knees thanking and praising God.

In case you think I'm a glutton for punishment, please know that I like my creature comforts as much as the next person. However, it is when I recognize God's perfect economy at work in the seemingly less-than-perfect moments of my life that I know His Kingdom is closer at hand.

As a spouse and parent, my path to holiness is populated with approximately three kajillion details that beckon me away from my own desires and toward those of the people closest to me. Real talk: I've found detaching from a "my way or the highway" mindset to be the hardest part of being a human in search of holiness.

It's easy to praise and thank God for His goodness when everything is going according to my plan. When there's money in the bank, when children obey, when the project is completed on time, when the noise level is tolerable, and when quality time with my spouse is frequent, then, praise the Lord.

But what about when I'm running on little to no sleep, my spouse just ran out the door without breakfast, the third spill of the morning lies on the dining room floor unattended just long enough for the dog to roll in it? How quick am I to high-five Jesus then?

When the diagnosis is dire, or the job is lost, or the chance for reconciliation with the friend appears impossible, do I cry out to my Heavenly Father as Job did: *the Lord gave and the Lord has taken away; blessed be the Name of the Lord* (Job 1:21)?

It has taken me a long while to learn that gratitude is as much a choice and an act of my free will as deciding to love, or forgive, or choose joy. I can complain about what I think I lack (which is usually control of my circumstances or my time), or I can choose to thank God for His infinite blessings: the miracle of indoor plumbing; clothes on our backs; warm food in our bellies; and small people who still allow me to hug and kiss them goodnight.

What would happen if I saw each interruption, every sidetrack, and all detours from my agenda not as distractions from the gift God offers, but as the gift itself? What if these inconveniences and struggles are God's clarion call for me to surrender to His loving embrace, and an opportunity to reflect that love to those around me?

Through God's living Word and His infinite mercy, I am beginning to see that which no less than canonized saints have declared—that everything is God's grace—God's gift—for us. Blessed be the Name of the Lord!

Everything is a grace, everything is the direct effect of our Father's love—difficulties, contradictions, humiliations, all the soul's miseries, her burdens, her needs— everything, because through them, she learns humility, realizes her weakness— Everything is a grace because everything is God's gift. Whatever be the character of life or its unexpected events—to the heart that loves, all is well.

(Saint Thérèse of Lisieux, *The Story of a Soul*)

HEATHER RENSHAW

THE LORD GAVE AND THE LORD HAS TAKEN AWAY; BLESSED BE THE NAME OF THE LORD

JOB 1:21

LECTIO DIVINA

LECTIO

Colossians 3:16-17
Paul provides examples of how to build each other up: by letting Christ's word dwell in us, by teaching and admonishing in wisdom, and by being thankful to God. We are to live in love as God's beloved children.

MEDITATIO

What personal message
does the text have for me?

ORATIO

What do I say to the Lord in
response to His word?

CONTEMPLATIO

What conversion of mind,
heart, and life is He asking
of me today?

How did I progress in living the Word today?

ACTIO

How will I make my life a gift for others in charity?

What does God want me to do today?

REPENT

Do you fail to give thanks in all circumstances, to see that His grace is present in all situations?

FORGIVE

Is there someone who misses the gift of you?

Who takes you for granted?

Forgive them and look to Jesus, who knows your worth.

GIVE THANKS

Today, let's only make a list of things for which we're grateful.

Linger longer over an accounting of His glorious gifts, the signs that He loves you.

PRAY

Lord,
open my eyes to
Your gifts in even
the smallest moments of my life.
Make me truly grateful.

the fourth week of lent

EVERY DAY THIS WEEK:

SCRIPTURE READINGS

ESSAY REFLECTION

LECTIO DIVINA

REPENT, FORGIVE, GIVE THANKS

PRAYER

MORE THIS WEEK:

WEEKLY SCRIPTURE MEMORY

WEEKLY SCRIPTURE MEMORY

FOURTH SUNDAY OF LENT

Here, we continue to memorize Colossians 3:12-17.

Over the course of Lent, we will commit to memory the entire passage Paul gives to the Colossians in order to tell them how to live a new life in the Lord. Taking it just a little bit at a time and building week after week, we can commit the passage to memory and—even better—we can hide it in our hearts.

COLOSSIANS 3:15

AND LET THE PEACE OF CHRIST RULE IN YOUR HEARTS, TO WHICH INDEED YOU WERE CALLED IN THE ONE BODY. AND BE THANKFUL.

let the

PEACE

- OF -

CHRIST

rule

in your

hearts.

COLOSSIANS 3:15

WEEKLY PLANS

SUNDAY

MONDAY

TUESDAY

WEDNESDAY

THURSDAY

FRIDAY

SATURDAY

PRAY + FAST + GIVE

sunday

MATTHEW 11:28-30

"Come to me, all you that are weary and are carrying heavy burdens, and I will give you rest. Take my yoke upon you, and learn from me; for I am gentle and humble in heart, and you will find rest for your souls. For my yoke is easy, and my burden is light."

FOR FURTHER CONTEMPLATION:

JOHN 7:37

PSALM 55:22

I'm sitting in the car outside the dance studio as I write. It's 27 degrees outside, the week before Christmas, and I'm siphoning wifi from the studio. Usually, when the girls are at dance I write in a coffee shop or at Whole Foods. I settle in and I'm mostly civilized about it. Not tonight. Tonight, there was basketball in addition to soccer, and there was an airport pickup, and there was physical therapy, and there is a writing deadline looming. My husband has been out of town for a week. I only have half an hour between dropping off at basketball and gathering girls from dance, not enough time to get settled into a coffee shop. Not enough time to sit comfortably at a table instead of balancing the laptop on my lap.

How did I get into this mess, squeezing in writing between a million other commitments? Why did I say "yes" again, even as I knew the absurdity of the deadline request? My pride told me that I could handle more than a person should handle, and gluttony wanted to gather every good part of this writing for myself, to guzzle it down in three short weeks because I truly love my work.

And here I sit, uncomfortably full. I do not sit here alone. All around the world tonight, men and women sit late at desks, making one more call, crossing one last thing off a list. We are overly full and we are desperately hungry.

We don't say no. Instead, we set ourselves up to feel inadequate as we strive to do tasks that we were never meant to do at all. We fill ourselves with opportunities and appointments and we empty ourselves of peace. We have lost our grasp on what our responsibilities truly are in God's Kingdom and have instead taken upon us a cross that was never meant to be borne.

Maybe this book and this deadline are His will for me. Maybe this is exactly what He wants me to do. If so, then I need to ask Him to help me to discern which other things on my list are not of His calling. Because He does not call me into the chaos. He calls me into peace.

God calls us into the peaceful presence of His Providence. He meets us every time, giving us adequate strength and grace to do His will. If we are stretched and broken, it's not of Him. Stretching to the breaking point is the pride yielding in pain.

He calls to us, the weary and the heavy-laden. He assures us that we can find genuine rest in Him. He beckons us away from frantic and chaotic and crazy-busy and asks us to be gentle and lowly in heart. We are soul weary and He is saying, Find me. Find stillness. Seek my will and say "no" to whatever is outside of it. There, see? That burden is light.

ELIZABETH FOSS

HE DOES NOT
CALL ME
INTO THE CHAOS.
HE CALLS ME
INTO
PEACE.

LECTIO DIVINA

LECTIO

Matthew 11:28-30
Jesus invites his disciples to follow and learn from him as the model of perfect obedience to God. In Matthew's Gospel, the contrast between the Old Covenant and the New Covenant offered by Jesus is an overriding theme; here, we see that Jesus offers not just physical rest, which is what the Old Covenant called for on the Sabbath, but soul rest, in doing the Father's will.

MEDITATIO

What personal message does the text have for me?

ORATIO

What do I say to the Lord in response to His word?

CONTEMPLATIO

What conversion of mind, heart, and life is He asking of me today?

How did I progress in living the Word today?

ACTIO

How will I make my life a gift for others in charity?

What does God want me to do today?

REPENT

Are you prioritizing your life according to God's will?

Do you neglect quiet time with God because you are agreeing to do things that fill you with worldly pleasure or acclamation?

Are you confused about which responsibilities are yours and which are God's?

Can you slow down and trust that God will provide everything you need?

FORGIVE

Is there someone who sucks you into chaos by demanding more of you than one person can manage?

Set your boundaries and then forgive him or her the sin of overestimating.

GIVE THANKS

Were there moments of rest today, moments when you were still and quiet?

Did you say "yes" to something you are sure is God's will for you?

Did you say "no" to something you know will crowd out something better?

PRAY

Slow me down, Lord.
Please bring peace to my heart.
Let me be content with the life You desire for me.
Help me to discern how You want me to use
the gift of time You've given me.

monday

2 CORINTHIANS 4:7-18

But we have this treasure in clay jars, so that it may be made clear that this extraordinary power belongs to God and does not come from us. We are afflicted in every way, but not crushed; perplexed, but not driven to despair; persecuted, but not forsaken; struck down, but not destroyed; always carrying in the body the death of Jesus, so that the life of Jesus may also be made visible in our bodies. For while we live, we are always being given up to death for Jesus' sake, so that the life of Jesus may be made visible in our mortal flesh. So death is at work in us, but life in you.

But just as we have the same spirit of faith that is in accordance with scripture—"I believed, and so I spoke"—we also believe, and so we speak, because we know that the one who raised the Lord Jesus will raise us also with Jesus, and will bring us with you into his presence. Yes, everything is for your sake, so that grace, as it extends to more and more people, may increase thanksgiving, to the glory of God.

So we do not lose heart. Even though our outer nature is wasting away, our inner nature is being renewed day by day. For this slight momentary affliction is preparing us for an eternal weight of glory beyond all measure, because we look not at what can be seen but at what cannot be seen; for what can be seen is temporary, but what cannot be seen is eternal.

FOR FURTHER CONTEMPLATION

ROMANS 7:15

2 CORINTHIANS 12:9

Prior to Confession, I used to pray through an examination of conscience and make a list of sins before entering the confessional. After I completed my penance, I would take a match to the paper and watch the sins give way to the flames. How cathartic to see a physical representation of the cleansing act of Confession. But then, I got lazy. The list seemed less necessary and more like a chore. I confess the same sins every time, so why bother to write them down?

I confess the same sins every time.

That was exactly my problem.

I had grown apathetic towards resolutions, towards the advice given to me by my confessor. And as a result, I fell back into the same traps over and over again.

Since arriving in this little British town of Street, Somerset, I've taken to the pavement as a way of self-care. Running is one of the rare activities in which I can completely give in to my thoughts. While exploring a new route last week, I turned the corner and was struck by a house covered in red ivy. England doesn't get autumn like Charlottesville does, but she certainly does her best. The ivy had begun to give way to winter, the whole house covered in what looked like licks of fire. I was struck by its beauty, by its alarming color.

I couldn't get it out of my mind the rest of the route, nor later that evening, nor the following day. Eventually it dawned on me: the ivy was attractive, but all-consuming.

I began to research ivy and identified it as Boston Ivy. It's harmless if kept in check, but can cause structural damage if left unattended.

And just like that, I realized why God had led me around the corner.

We are human, so we err. We indulge when we should ration. We snap when we should practice patience. We turn away from Him when we should run toward.

Afflicted, but not crushed.

Perplexed, but not driven to despair.

Persecuted, but not forsaken.

Struck down, but not destroyed.

We are overcome by the same shortcomings. By the same character flaws. By the same sins. They come and go like the seasons. And what do we make of the rotation of seasons, the return every year of winter's cold kiss, the bounty of fall fading into slow decay?

We do not lose heart.

Even though our outer nature is wasting away, our inner nature is being renewed day by day.

You, dear reader, have this book open as we move out of winter. You are witness to the blossoming, the opening of spring like a blooming peony. You see the rejuvenation of the world as we approach the celebration of the resurrection of our Savior.

Yes, we live in a broken and wounded world. But we have strong masonry. He built us in His own image, with bricks strong enough to keep out even the most invasive sins. The ivy may sit on our skin, but through Him and with Him, we have the protection needed to keep the grace inside alive.

CARLY BUCKHOLZ

> **EVEN THOUGH**
> **OUR *OUTER NATURE***
> **IS WASTING AWAY,**
> **OUR *INNER NATURE***
> **IS BEING RENEWED**
> **DAY BY DAY.**

LECTIO DIVINA

LECTIO

2 Corinthians 4:7-18
Second Corinthians responds to developments in Corinth since the sending of First Corinthians, in particular to the charges of some false apostles who were trying to discredit Paul.

MEDITATIO

What personal message does the text have for me?

ORATIO

What do I say to the Lord in response to His word?

CONTEMPLATIO

What conversion of mind, heart, and life is He asking of me today?

How did I progress in living the Word today?

ACTIO

How will I make my life a gift for others in charity?

What does God want me to do today?

REPENT

Do you despair, thinking that you will never truly conquer sin, never grow in holiness?

Do you doubt the power of God to heal your broken places?

FORGIVE

Is someone impatient with your imperfections?

Forgive and know God uses those imperfections to bless others and make His glory known.

GIVE THANKS

Can you see the big picture, the places where we grow in wisdom even as we grow more frail, the wide open spaces of vulnerability where He lets us meet other people?

Those are the God places in our lives; be grateful for them.

PRAY

Lord,
let Your light
shine through
the cracks
in my broken
places.

ABOVE ALL | FOURTH WEEK OF LENT

tuesday

ROMANS 6:1-14

What then are we to say? Should we continue in sin that grace may abound? By no means! How can we who died to sin go on living in it? Do you not know that all of us who have been baptized into Christ Jesus were baptized into his death? Therefore we have been buried with him by baptism into death, so that, just as Christ was raised from the dead by the glory of the Father, so we too might walk in newness of life.

For if we have been united with him in a death like his, we shall certainly be united with him in a resurrection like his. We know that our old self was crucified with him so that the body of sin might be destroyed, and we might no longer be enslaved to sin. For whoever has died is freed from sin. But if we have died with Christ, we believe that we shall also live with him. We know that Christ, being raised from the dead, will never die again; death no longer has dominion over him. The death he died, he died to sin, once for all; but the life he lives, he lives to God. So you also must consider yourselves dead to sin and alive to God in Christ Jesus.

Therefore, do not let sin exercise dominion in your mortal bodies, to make you obey their passions. No longer present your members to sin as instruments of wickedness, but present yourselves to God as those who have been brought from death to life, and present your members to God as instruments of righteousness. For sin will have no dominion over you, since you are not under law but under grace.

FOR FURTHER CONTEMPLATION:

GALATIANS 2:20

ROMANS 5:18-21

What does it look like when you realize that you've been viewing God the wrong way your whole life? For me it looked like this:

I was beginning to homeschool my two oldest daughters for the first time. They were five years old and four years old, in kindergarten and preschool, and we began our day with some prayer and a little reading from a catechism booklet. They were totally enthralled by the lesson and followed it up with more questions than I had anticipated. In the end, the topic they were most interested in was the resurrection of the body at the second coming—just your typical, light, preschool and kindergarten discussion.

By the time we got to the end of that conversation, I was nearing my first panic attack. I was attempting to explain to my eager and innocent daughters that our bodies are created good, and that we are daughters of God, saved by Christ who enables us to enter into His resurrection by His own death and rising from the dead, but what I realized during my explanation is that I did not really believe all that I was telling them.

At that moment I came face to face with what I had been telling myself for years and years: that God is an avenging God who sees only my sins, that He is in heaven waiting for me to inevitably fall into sin, that I am a terrible person who does little more than sin, and that there is no way God loves me enough to save me, and to want me with Him for all eternity, body and soul.

As you can imagine, years of this sort of self-talk takes a long time to reverse, and I still work every day to combat this false understanding of who our Lord is and who I am to Him. What I had missed for so long were the most fundamental truths about God that I should've taken away from my many years of Catholic schooling: that I am a daughter of God, that God loved me first, that Christ died and rose for me. As a result, I had missed out on being able to revel each day in the great joy that comes from realizing the truth of these things.

Saint Paul says, "For if we have been united with him in a death like his, we will certainly be united with him in a resurrection like his." (Romans 6:5) And this resurrection presupposes a great love for each of us by a good God who desires to spend eternity with us.

I began to repeat to myself daily that I am a beloved daughter of God.

"We know that our old self was crucified with him so that the body of sin might be destroyed, and we might no longer be enslaved to sin." (Romans 6:6)

In many ways my "old self" was my "self" who did not believe that I am a passionately-loved daughter of God, and that God's love is not wearied by my sins. It's not that I should go on committing sins and presuming His constant forgiveness, but that my fallen nature should not serve to discourage me. Instead, my weakness makes me all the more dependent on the great love and mercies that flow from the cross and resurrection.

ANA HAHN

I began to repeat to myself daily that I am a beloved daughter of God.

LECTIO DIVINA

Romans 6:1-14

Paul wrote his letter to the Romans from Corinth in the winter of 57 A.D. to introduce himself to the Christians in Rome. The letter is hailed as one of the greatest works of Christian theology. The letter's main theme is the salvation of the world through Christ.

MEDITATIO

What personal message
does the text have for me?

ORATIO

What do I say to the Lord in
response to His word?

CONTEMPLATIO

What conversion of mind,
heart, and life is He asking
of me today?

How did I progress in living the Word today?

ACTIO

How will I make my life a gift for others in charity?

What does God want me to do today?

REPENT

Do I hold my sins in my heart and refuse to accept Christ's forgiveness?

FORGIVE

Forgive yourself today.

GIVE THANKS

Today, just rest and be grateful that "sin will have no dominion over you, since you are not under law but under grace." (Romans 6:14)

Pray that God gives you the strength and faith you need to open yourself to His grace.

PRAY

Thank You Jesus,
for Your work on the cross.
Thank You for dying to bring me life.
Thank You for letting me live in Your grace,
for showing me a way back to Your shelter,
though every day I stumble and fall.

wednesday

"When the Son of Man comes in his glory, and all the angels with him, then he will sit on the throne of his glory. All the nations will be gathered before him, and he will separate people one from another as a shepherd separates the sheep from the goats, and he will put the sheep at his right hand and the goats at the left. Then the king will say to those at his right hand, 'Come, you that are blessed by my Father, inherit the kingdom prepared for you from the foundation of the world; for I was hungry and you gave me food, I was thirsty and you gave me something to drink, I was a stranger and you welcomed me, I was naked and you gave me clothing, I was sick and you took care of me, I was in prison and you visited me.' Then the righteous will answer him, 'Lord, when was it that we saw you hungry and gave you food, or thirsty and gave you something to drink? And when was it that we saw you a stranger and welcomed you, or naked and gave you clothing? And when was it that we saw you sick or in prison and visited you?' And the king will answer them, 'Truly I tell you, just as you did it to one of the least of these who are members of my family, you did it to me.' Then he will say to those at his left hand, 'You that are accursed, depart from me into the eternal fire prepared for the devil and his angels; for I was hungry and you gave me no food, I was thirsty and you gave me nothing to drink, I was a stranger and you did not welcome me, naked and you did not give me clothing, sick and in prison and you did not visit me.' Then they also will answer, 'Lord, when was it that we saw you hungry or thirsty or a stranger or naked or sick or in prison, and did not take care of you?' Then he will answer them, 'Truly I tell you, just as you did not do it to one of the least of these, you did not do it to me.' And these will go away into eternal punishment, but the righteous into eternal life."

FOR FURTHER CONTEMPLATION:

1 JOHN 3:18

GALATIANS 6:7-10

JAMES 2:15-17

Do you see Him sitting there on His glorious throne? In my imagination, the Lord of Judgment looks like a cross between Gandalf and Dumbledore. He is majestic and wise, at once imposing and approachable. This is the moment upon which all eternity hangs. He has but one criterion.

Love.

Have you put on love and lived as one is who are deeply in love with the Lord, so deeply that it overflows from your soul in genuine and personal ways to the many people He has very deliberately put in your path?

Those everyday people in your everyday life are the people He entrusted to you. Did you love them well? To put on love each day and go out into the world as new creations in Christ is not the doing of good deeds, it's the loving of real souls, it's the work of extending the friendship of Christ to the real people He puts in our paths. Our God asks us to clothe our neighbors with His love—to put love upon them even as we take it upon ourselves. He wants us to look beyond the externals of race or status or distinction or education, to see the soul, and to love it with God's own love.

This is it, His standard of judgment: How well did you love?

Sometimes, it is hard to discern the good to which He calls us; it's hard to know where to invest our time and our treasure for the kingdom of God. Christ doesn't call us to a life of easy answers or easy labor. Instead, He calls us to love one another. And as we approach Good Friday, we are increasingly aware that He died and rose again to forgive our failures in answering this call and to make mercy possible.

We are called to love. Love is rooted in humility. Love is sacrificial and self-donating. In its purest form, love pours a joyful passion for Jesus Christ into the heart of one's neighbor (or spouse or child or sister or friend). When we love in Christ's name, we show the mercy of a God who stretched out His arms on an instrument of torture in order to breathe His very being into us and bring us to Himself.

The kingdom of God is vast and expansive. I doubt I will ever be called to ladle soup in the jungles of South America. I doubt I'll be called to bind the wounded in war-torn Africa. But I will be called nearly daily to feed my children at a dining table in suburban Virginia, and I will spend countless hours both rocking feverish babies and soothing broken hearts. This is my encounter with humanity. Yours might be very similar, or it might look altogether different. This is His work for us, the work we accepted when we accepted the grace of His work on the cross. This is our path to sanctity: to love with our whole hearts.

ELIZABETH FOSS

LECTIO DIVINA

LECTIO

Matthew 25:31-46
Jesus is speaking to His disciples on the Mount of Olives a few days before His arrest and death. In this accounting of the Last Judgment, Jesus identifies Himself with all men, especially the poor and the afflicted. When we serve them, we serve Christ. However, if we ignore the poor and afflicted, we ignore Christ.

MEDITATIO

What personal message
does the text have for me?

ORATIO

What do I say to the Lord in
response to His word?

CONTEMPLATIO

What conversion of mind,
heart, and life is He asking
of me today?

How did I progress in living the Word today?

ACTIO

How will I make my life a gift for others in charity?
What does God want me to do today?

REPENT

Have you seized all the little opportunities He has offered in your everyday life in an ordinary world to love your neighbor by being Jesus' hands and feet?

FORGIVE

You have looked for love, for consolation, for comfort, and you have been turned away.

Forgive the missed opportunity.

Know that God loves you always, with the fullness of His sorrowful heart.

GIVE THANKS

For all the people who have shown you the love of Christ, be truly grateful.

PRAY

Father God,
Thank You for setting the standard of love,
for showing me what it is to
pour out one's whole life for another.
Help me to meet the standard
You set for me.

thursday

PROVERBS 16:24

Pleasant words are like a honeycomb,
sweetness to the soul and health to the
body.

FOR FURTHER CONTEMPLATION:

PROVERBS 12:18

PROVERBS 26:20-21

For the next three days, we are going to apologize well. Hopefully, by now, you've confessed the sins you've committed against God. You've repented. You've heard the words of absolution.

Now, together, we're going to do the hard work of turning to the people closest to us and saying, "Have mercy on me, a sinner. Please?"

Before we carefully examine what an apology is, let's look at what it isn't. An apology is not "I'm sorry you got upset." That's the pride holding on. That's what someone says when they assign blame to someone else. Instead, apology claims responsibility. "I'm sorry. I hurt you, and I understand how I hurt you."

A recent study* delineated six steps to a good apology

1. **Expression of regret**
2. **Explanation of what went wrong**
3. **Acknowledgment of responsibility**
4. **Declaration of repentance**
5. **Offer of repair**
6. **Request for forgiveness**

Of those six steps, the most important was claiming responsibility, followed closely by sincerely attempting to repair the hurt. John Gottman, an expert in healthy marriages, has spent his lifetime promoting the repair attempt. In relationships, the importance of a sincere apology and the effort towards repair cannot be overstated. A healthy apology begins with the understanding that you've done something wrong, and then it moves quickly to the careful articulation of what you've done. Be honest. Call out the whole sin with sincere courage; resist the urge to offer a weak apology for a small component of a bigger problem. Resist the urge to charm your way out of true, mature expression that you've made a mistake that caused someone else pain.

There's something else an apology is not. Sometimes, we are so proud and so vain and so sensitive to what others think about us, that we lie when we utter the words of apology. We apologize for things that are not our fault or for which we are not sorry because we hate conflict more than we love truth. An apology is not a lie.

An apology is not a chance to dig up past wounds or to justify bad behavior. Keep your apology short, sincere, and to the point. Say the actual words "I'm sorry," and state the offense. Ask for forgiveness. And then let it go. Don't throw wood on the fire of strife. Douse it with sincere repentance.

If you are an over-apologizer, make a promise to God and the person to whom you are most likely to throw out an insincere apology: No more. No more sacrificing truth in a relationship for the sake of false peace.

As difficult as it is to put pen to paper and admit even to yourself, there are likely times in your life where you have really messed up an apology. It is entirely possible that the errors you've made have caused deep wounds and may have left ugly scars.

It's never too late.

Here, now, sketch out a plan for making amends. If you must, write a letter taking responsibility. If at all possible, though, let that letter be only for the purpose of organizing your thoughts as you resolve to make things right in person.

*(https://www.sciencedaily.com/releases/2016/04/160412091111.htm)

ELIZABETH FOSS

DON'T THROW WOOD ON THE FIRE OF STRIFE. DOUSE IT WITH SINCERE REPENTANCE.

LECTIO DIVINA

LECTIO

Proverbs 16:24
Proverbs is one of the Wisdom Books of the Old Testament. It's a collection of sayings of King Solomon and other Israelite wise men and scribes on various subjects. The book is intended to impart lessons for wise living, and contrasts the practice of wisdom against the practice of folly.

MEDITATIO

What personal message does the text have for me?

ORATIO

What do I say to the Lord in response to His word?

CONTEMPLATIO

What conversion of mind, heart, and life is He asking of me today?

How did I progress in living the Word today?

ACTIO

How will I make my life a gift for others in charity?
What does God want me to do today?

REPENT

Have you failed to apologize promptly, stubbornly digging into your own self-righteousness and sacrificing genuine reconciliation?

Have you apologized insincerely, shifting the responsibility from your own failings and blaming the hurt on the victim of your sins?

Have you dug up old offenses and opened old wounds in the heat of argument?

Have you ever apologized for something about which you were not sorry or you had no fault, only because you wanted to gain the false peace that comes with avoiding conflict?

FORGIVE

You have done this, again and again. Throughout these Lenten days, you've forgiven without being asked. Again, let go of those old offenses.

GIVE THANKS

Apologies sincerely offered are beautiful ways to repair a relationship. Give thanks for every one of those and for the people who are able to render them.

PRAY

Please, Lord, make me humble.
Help me to see how my pride has blinded me
to the times I've needed to utter a sincere, contrite apology.
As much as it hurts and as humiliating as it may be,
let me reach out and begin to heal the relationships
I've hurt by failing to honestly say "I'm sorry."

friday

MATTHEW 5:23-24

So when you are offering your gift at the altar,
if you remember that your brother or sister
has something against you, leave your gift
before the altar and go; first be reconciled to
your brother or sister, and then come and
offer your gift.

FOR FURTHER CONTEMPLATION:

GALATIANS 6:7

2 CORINTHIANS 7:10-11

PROVERBS 6:16-19

God wants us to apologize. The inability to apologize is stubborn pride, and it's one of the most useful tools the devil has to destroy relationships. When we apologize sincerely, we go beyond confessing we were wrong; we ask forgiveness and we attempt repair.

Stand firm in your contrition. Don't make excuses. Don't shift the blame. Sometimes, our carelessness can cause true and deep pain in the people we love. Apologies unsaid are wicked seeds sown. They grow roots and bear bitter fruit for years to come. The longer they go unsaid, the more tenacious and far-reaching they grow, until they are choking every good thing around them.

Remember, you're not sorry you got caught (well, you probably are, but that's not the point). You're sorry you caused pain. Apology means that your well-developed conscience understands that something you did hurt someone else, and now you grieve over what you have wrought.

If you're the kind of person who rarely apologizes, take a good look at why.

Is it because you genuinely believe that you are rarely wrong? Pray for clarity here, for insight and wisdom. Pray that God develops in you a keener sense of your own propensity for sin, because if you really believe that you're rarely the person who should apologize, you have a very serious pride problem.

Maybe you struggle to apologize because you are afraid. You fear that the vulnerability that comes with apology weakens you in the eyes of the person you've offended or that it will weaken the position of strength you hold in the relationship. On both accounts, nothing could be further from the truth. A healthy person will accept an apology as a sign of strength, of genuine courage. Apology increases your value in a relationship; it doesn't take from it. Further, too many missed apologies can erode at your value so grievously that, over time, very little respect remains (if any).

But maybe you hesitate to apologize because you're the person who rarely understands that your actions can hurt other people. Maybe you are so self-absorbed or emotionally immature that you lack the empathy necessary for genuine remorse. Pray for empathy. Pray for empathy for all your relationships. Pray that your own suffering will soften your heart towards the suffering of someone else. Jesus entered into our suffering. He didn't offer sympathetic words from on high; He came to us to be beaten and bloodied and cursed and humiliated. He came to feel pain so that we could feel pain for one another and then do something about it.

It takes courage to pray for empathy, particularly when a relationship is being stressed, which is a very good time to utter those prayers. Empathy will open your soul to someone else's pain. You will feel the pain and the shame and the rejection and the loss that someone else feels. In the case where an apology is needed, you will feel the sorrow that comes with knowing you caused that pain. You will stand at the foot of the cross, look up, and know you are responsible for the horror you see there.

With even the slightest glimmer of understanding that you've hurt someone, step forward with sincere words of responsibility and contrition. Ask to be forgiven. Offer to make it better. If it's not totally obvious what needs to be done, ask what you can do. Brainstorm together about the path forward into complete reconciliation.

If you take nothing else from this Lenten season, take this: Christ wants you to kneel in sorrow and ask to be forgiven.

ELIZABETH FOSS

Christ wants you to kneel in sorrow and ask to be forgiven.

LECTIO DIVINA

Matthew 5:23-24

This passage, from the Sermon on the Mount, is another example of Jesus' call for us to aspire to deep holiness, which involves how we treat others. Jesus wants us to be reconciled with each other, not to be at odds with one another.

MEDITATIO

What personal message does the text have for me?

ORATIO

What do I say to the Lord in response to His word?

CONTEMPLATIO

What conversion of mind, heart, and life is He asking of me today?

How did I progress in living the Word today?

ACTIO

How will I make my life a gift for others in charity?
What does God want me to do today?

REPENT

Do you genuinely believe that you are rarely wrong?

Do you withhold apology because you think it weakens you?

Do you miss the cues that you have hurt, or are hurting, someone else?

FORGIVE

Are there people in your life who fail to be empathetic?

Forgive them.

GIVE THANKS

You've been given the grace needed to apologize sincerely. Thank God for that.

PRAY

Thank You, Lord,
for the gift of genuine apology,
both those You enable me to offer
and those I receive.

ABOVE ALL | FOURTH WEEK OF LENT

saturday

GENESIS 50:19-21

But Joseph said to them, "Do not be afraid! Am I in the place of God? Even though you intended to do harm to me, God intended it for good, in order to preserve a numerous people, as he is doing today. So have no fear; I myself will provide for you and your little ones." In this way he reassured them, speaking kindly to them.

FOR FURTHER CONTEMPLATION:

MATTHEW 6:14-15

2 CHRONICLES 7:14

MATTHEW 18:21-22

The beautiful thing about an apology well offered is that, many times, it creates fertile ground for relationship growth. God is clear about what He desires for us in the moments after an apology. He wants us to forgive. He's adamant, actually, and we will be forgiven as we forgive. That's a big deal.

The story of Joseph is such a beautiful example of how He can work with humility and forgiveness. Joseph's brothers left him for dead at the bottom of a well. They caused unimaginable pain to their father, who thought he'd lost his son. They were just plain mean, among countless other things. And they were brought to repentance only when they discovered that Joseph was the very man who could save them from starvation. Theirs was not a perfect apology.

But Joseph forgave them. Not only that, he understood the limit of his forgiveness and God's capacity to bring great good out of a bad situation. Joseph allowed his brothers to own their transgressions, but he didn't stubbornly dig in his heels and seek vengeance. Instead, he allowed himself to be used by God to save their lives. Every time someone apologizes, and asks forgiveness, the offended party has an opportunity to breathe new life into that person's heart. Think on that a few minutes. Pray on it. Are you life-giving when you are on the receiving end of an apology?

Christ tells us we need to be willing to genuinely forgive over and over again. Further, He acknowledges that sometimes we do forgive and all is right for awhile, and then something happens that re-opens the old wound. The hurt resurfaces, and with it, the opportunity to forgive. Further, we must forgive every time it comes to mind, for as long as we remember.

Often, it's in our best interest to remember. Forgiving isn't the same as forgetting. Instead, someone else's sins can hold valuable lessons for us — lessons in navigating the tricky waters of complicated relationships, lessons in boundaries, lessons in learning to replace foolishness with wisdom.

Remembering isn't for revenge. (Romans 12:19) It's important to relinquish completely the desire to retaliate. Our suffering pales in comparison to what they will face if they don't repent and amend their ways. Even in the hurt, we soften our hearts for compassion.

But compassion does not ask us to let ourselves be victims again. On the contrary, we have a responsibility to protect ourselves from harm. Just as we refuse to put ourselves in physical harm, we protect ourselves from emotional harm. It is entirely possible to forgive someone while at the same time constructing a strong and sturdy boundary against further pain.

That boundary is a mercy to the one who inflicted the pain, too. If we allow ourselves to be victims over and over again, then the people who harm us associate no logical consequence for the damage they have done. Forgiveness that also results in the consequence of a boundary is not incomplete forgiveness. Protecting oneself from further harm is good self-care, and it's a good idea to be kind and gentle to ourselves when we've been hurt. When we forgive, our hearts are transformed. Protecting that healing heart is both prudent and kind.

When you are the one apologizing, there exists the very real possibility that you will offer a sincere apology and it will not be forgiven. Give that to God. Only He can heal the hurt.

And there exists the possibility that you will be called upon to forgive something for which the offender never offers an apology. God's got that one, too. He can, and will, give you the grace and strength to move beyond the wounds inflicted by other people and He will heal them—completely.

This stuff of apology and forgiveness is not small stuff. Truly, this is the heart of the Easter story. It is dying and rising again. It is why He came and why He suffered, and how He offers hope. On this side of heaven, the closest we can get to resurrection is a healthy relationship where we repent and ask forgiveness with our whole hearts and we forgive and are forgiven in kind.

ELIZABETH FOSS

LECTIO DIVINA

LECTIO

Genesis 50:19-21

Genesis, which means "origins" or "birth", is the first book of the Bible and demonstrates how God guides human history according to His own salvific purposes. According to Christian and Jewish tradition, Genesis was written by Moses in the 15th or 13th century B.C. In this passage, Joseph forgives his treacherous brothers who sold him into slavery in Egypt, stating that what they intended for harm, God intended for good.

MEDITATIO

What personal message does the text have for me?

ORATIO

What do I say to the Lord in response to His word?

CONTEMPLATIO

What conversion of mind, heart, and life is He asking of me today?

How did I progress in living the Word today?

ACTIO

How will I make my life a gift for others in charity?

What does God want me to do today?

REPENT

Do you bear wrongs patiently?
Do you withhold forgiveness
while you wait for the perfect
apology?

Are you willing to forgive the
same sin over and over?

FORGIVE

What is that offense that you've
forgiven seventy-seven times,
but still keeps coming to mind?
Forgive it again.

GIVE THANKS

Have you received a sincere
apology and had the grace to
forgive?

PRAY

Dear Lord,
I beg You to breathe grace
into my relationships.
Allow me to experience the joy
of both apology and forgiveness.

fifth week of lent

EVERY DAY THIS WEEK:

SCRIPTURE READINGS

ESSAY REFLECTION

LECTIO DIVINA

REPENT, RESTORE, GIVE THANKS

PRAYER

MORE THIS WEEK:

WEEKLY SCRIPTURE MEMORY

WEEKLY SCRIPTURE MEMORY

FIFTH SUNDAY OF LENT

Here, we continue to memorize Colossians 3:12-17

Over the course of Lent, we will commit to memory the entire passage Paul gives to Colossians in order to tell them how to live a new life in the Lord. Taking it just a little bit at a time and building week after week, we can commit the passage to memory and—even better—we can hide it in our hearts.

COLOSSIANS 3:16

LET THE WORD OF CHRIST DWELL IN YOU RICHLY; TEACH AND ADMONISH ONE ANOTHER IN ALL WISDOM; AND WITH GRATITUDE IN YOUR HEARTS SING PSALMS, HYMNS, AND SPIRITUAL SONGS TO GOD.

let the
WORD
OF CHRIST
dwell in you
richly.
COLOSSIANS 3:16

WEEKLY PLANS

SUNDAY

MONDAY

TUESDAY

WEDNESDAY

THURSDAY

FRIDAY

SATURDAY

PRAY + FAST + GIVE

1 CORINTHIANS 9:24-27

Do you not know that in a race all the runners compete, but only one receives the prize? Run in such a way that you may win it. Athletes exercise self-control in all things; they do it to receive a perishable wreath, but we an imperishable one. So I do not run aimlessly, nor do I box as though beating the air; but I punish my body and enslave it, so that after proclaiming to others I myself should not be disqualified.

FOR FURTHER CONTEMPLATION:

HEBREWS 4:1-6

JOHN 15:19

ROMANS 12:2

1 PETER 2:9

HEBREWS 4:7-13

NEHEMIAH 9:18-20

It's a classic conversation where two or more Catholics are gathered on a Sunday during Lent: Do you take a break and allow yourself the things you "gave up", or do you keep the fast all the way through Lent, even on Sundays?

I'll let you debate that amongst yourselves.

What we do know is that, throughout the year, every Sunday is a little Easter and every Mass is an occasion of joy. Even if you choose to maintain your Lenten fast throughout the entire season without taking a break on Sundays, do not be sad today. Today is the Lord's Day, set apart for you by Him. Rejoice in the Lord and join your hearts with the glad hearts of the faithful all over the world as they worship today. Every Sunday, God gives us a glimpse of heaven. And in heaven we will rest in Him. Rest.

I live in a house full of very serious athletes. I watch them train with diligence and single-mindedness and it's easy to understand Saint Paul's analogy. But it's also easy to see something else. It's easy to see what happens when the athletic contest becomes a golden calf. I can see what happens when athletes over-train and overuse their muscles, when they lose sight of the real reason we run the race. My checkbook bears witness to the ruin as I log one copay after another at orthopedists and physical therapists. When we train to run as to win, we also must train to rest.

In order to run as to win the race, we have to discipline ourselves to stop running, too. We have to know that self-discipline means knowing when to feast and when to fast, and at either end of the spectrum to avoid extremes which endanger our bodies or our souls. We live in a fast-paced world. We go and go and go to the point of exhaustion. God calls to us on a Sunday and says, "Come to me, all you that are weary and are carrying heavy burdens, and I will give you rest." (Matthew 11:28)

Sundays remind us that we are a people set apart. We gather in community to worship and that sets us apart physically in the shelter of our churches, where Christ Himself nourishes us. In community, on Sundays, we are animated by the Lord. He fills our souls, and that filling is what propels us forward into the world as Christians.

Further, we then move forward into the world, each one of us doing soul work and animating the places where we live for Christ. We do the ordinary work of our ordinary days, lit from within by an extraordinary force. Sundays of worship and rest feed the fires of our souls. And it is that warmth and light we give to the people we meet, transforming the culture for Christ.

Your soul needs to rest and be fed. Truly, truly observe the Sabbath today.

Today is a day for rejoicing in rest.

ELIZABETH FOSS

TODAY
IS A DAY
FOR
REJOICING
IN REST.

LECTIO DIVINA

LECTIO

1 Corinthians 9:24-27
Today's selection from First Corinthians compares the spiritual life to athletic competition. Just as athletes must train their bodies to achieve victory and physical excellence, Christians must also train themselves in the spiritual life to reach the eternal reward of Heaven.

MEDITATIO

What personal message does the text have for me?

ORATIO

What do I say to the Lord in response to His word?

CONTEMPLATIO

What conversion of mind, heart, and life is He asking of me today?

How did I progress in living the Word today?

ACTIO

How will I make my life a gift for others in charity?

What does God want me to do today?

REPENT

Do you run roughshod over the Lord's day, working as if there is nothing special about it?

Do you miss Mass because the schedule crowds it out?

RESTORE

Today, take notes on the homily.

Use this space to let the Holy Spirit run through your fingers onto the page and into your soul.

GIVE THANKS

Praise God for the gift of the Mass.

Praise God for those moments of this day which were restful and restorative; number them

PRAY

Slow me down, Lord.
Help me to gently brake,
lest I am forced to a screeching halt.
Show me the quiet,
restful joys that You
intend for me.

monday

EXODUS 19:4-6A

You have seen what I did to the Egyptians, and how I bore you on eagles' wings and brought you to myself. Now therefore, if you obey my voice and keep my covenant, you shall be my treasured possession out of all the people. Indeed, the whole earth is mine, but you shall be for me a priestly kingdom and a holy nation.

FOR FURTHER CONTEMPLATION:

ROMANS 12:1-2

What's the first thing you did this morning? Even before your feet hit the floor? Did you offer the day to God?

In every day, moment by moment, God sends us cues to love one another, sends you cues specific to your unique life which, if you take them, lead you to love His people well. But we miss them. We get absorbed in the daily grind of details of living. The vortex of this age of information and instant response transforms us into frenzied beings who bounce from one thing to the next, missing the essence of one another in the transactions.

Often, we multi-task. Or we think we multi-task. We think we can listen to a child and answer an email from a colleague simultaneously. We think we can scroll through recipes and listen to our spouse's recounting of the day. The truth is, we can't. When we try to do two things at once, we do neither one well. When we rush headlong into the day, assuming God will tune to whatever frequency we're already moving along, we don't hear Him. And then we miss the chance to unite ourselves with Him.

Beginning today, ask for help transforming your mind so that you are finely tuned to God's best for you. I'm sharing my favorite morning offering with you today. Begin there, or with one of your choosing.

Then, take all your ordinary moments, the seemingly random components of your everyday life—cooking and eating, commuting and shopping, walking and waiting, tending and teaching—and give them to God over and over, with every unique gesture. Offer Him your coming and going, your pausing to rest, trusting His mercy to conform them to Himself. Focus on Him, just for a moment, but over many moments of your day.

As you move about life in the culture, resist becoming mindlessly enculturated. You belong to the city of God! Fix your attention on Him. Let Him transform you from within; let Him make your soul more and more like the image of Himself it was created to be. He can change you from the inside out, beginning today, making you sensitive to all the little moments that are opportunities for union with Christ.

Well-formed spiritual maturity bears the fruit of peace that comes with walking hand-in-hand with the Lord. Instead of those lofty New Year's resolution-type

Lenten offerings, dedicate these last couple of weeks to an unrestrained offer of yourself. This offering is both bigger and smaller. It's bigger because you hold nothing back from Him. You're all in. You're giving Him everything at every moment. It's smaller because you and He do this together, little moment by little moment, moving closer to matching His cadence with every small beat of your heart.

ELIZABETH FOSS

LET HIM TRANSFORM YOU FROM WITHIN; LET HIM MAKE YOUR SOUL MORE AND MORE LIKE THE IMAGE OF HIMSELF IT WAS CREATED TO BE.

LECTIO DIVINA

LECTIO

Exodus 19:4-6a

Exodus, the second book of the Bible, was also written by Moses. The book focuses mostly on the relationship between God and Moses, who brings the people out of slavery in Egypt and is given the law on Mount Sinai. *Exodos* is Greek for "departure" or "going out". The book could have been written any time between 1445-1406 B.C. Here, God has called Moses up Mount Sinai to give him the law.

MEDITATIO

What personal message does the text have for me?

ORATIO

What do I say to the Lord in response to His word?

CONTEMPLATIO

What conversion of mind, heart, and life is He asking of me today?

How did I progress in living the Word today?

ACTIO

How will I make my life a gift for others in charity?
What does God want me to do today?

REPENT

Do you offer God all the little details of your life or do you stubbornly hold onto some illusion of control?

Do you pray about the little details?

Do you listen carefully to the promptings of the Holy Spirit and ask Him to show you how to sanctify your daily round?

RESTORE

How will you cue yourself to take a breath repeatedly throughout the day and remember to offer the day to God?

Light a candle? Highlight times in your planner? Put post-it notes by your light switches? Set alarms on your phone?

GIVE THANKS

How did God make His presence known in the details of your day today, both within your heart and in the lives of the people you love?

Can you see that every moment matters to Him?

PRAY

O Lord,
grant that with Your peace
I may greet all that this day is to bring.
Grant me grace to surrender myself
completely to Your Holy Will.
In every hour of this day instruct me
and guide me in all things.
Teach me to accept tranquilly
whatever tidings I may receive during this day,
in the firm belief that Your Holy Will governs all.
Govern my thoughts and feelings
in all that I do and say.
When unforeseen things occur,
let me not forget that all is sent by You.
Teach me to behave sincerely
and reasonably toward everyone,
so that I may bring confusion and sorrow to no one.
Bestow on me, O Lord, strength to endure
the fatigue of the day and to bear my part in its events.
Guide my will and teach me to pray, to believe, to suffer,
to forgive and to love. Amen.

—St. John Kronstadt, of the Eastern Orthodox tradition

tuesday

What good is it, my brothers and sisters, if you say you have faith but do not have works? Can faith save you? If a brother or sister is naked and lacks daily food, and one of you says to them, "Go in peace; keep warm and eat your fill," and yet you do not supply their bodily needs, what is the good of that? So faith by itself, if it has no works, is dead.

But someone will say, "You have faith and I have works." Show me your faith apart from your works, and I by my works will show you my faith. You believe that God is one; you do well. Even the demons believe—and shudder. Do you want to be shown, you senseless person, that faith apart from works is barren? Was not our ancestor Abraham justified by works when he offered his son Isaac on the altar? You see that faith was active along with his works, and faith was brought to completion by the works. Thus the scripture was fulfilled that says, "Abraham believed God, and it was reckoned to him as righteousness," and he was called the friend of God. You see that a person is justified by works and not by faith alone.

FOR FURTHER CONTEMPLATION:

JOEL 2:12-13

PSALM 46:10

If you are holding this book in your hands, chances are good that you're committed to doing good things. You are well-intentioned. You want to do what is right, to be sure that you have good works to show. You have taken to heart the admonition that faith without works is dead.

But works without faith are pretty dead, too. Works without faith puff us up, make us feel good about ourselves, exalt us in front of our friends and neighbors. Works without faith are the stuff of pride.

We are not saved by our works. We are saved by the work of our merciful God on the cross. We are saved by the grace of God, poured out for us in an exorbitant act of mercy that allows us to work with grace.

Sometimes, we get so caught up in "doing the right thing" that we fall prey to the idea that if we just follow the right rules and act in the right way, we earn a place in heaven. Sometimes, we focus so hard on James' insistence that works are right and necessary, that we miss the first part. James begins with the assumption that a person has faith.

Are you going through the motions—doing and doing—but missing the relationship? God wants all of you. He wants you to know Him intimately. He is a jealous lover, calling you from the cares of the world into the embrace of His being. He wants to reveal Himself to you as the most trustworthy, reliable source of life and love in a world that twists in the wind every day.

God wants you to open your Bible this morning, and tomorrow, and next week, and next month. God wants to speak into your heart every day for the rest of your life and He wants you to be still and listen. Let the first thing you do for the Lord be to listen to the Lord.

It is the Word that is the same yesterday, today, and tomorrow. It is Him to whom you can return at any moment of any day and night and find solace and strength. It is faith in this singular, holy relationship with the Creator of your soul that will animate your works and sanctify your moments.

Works without faith are dead. God doesn't want you to go through the motions. He wants your faith in Him to be the force that makes the motions happen. Know Him.

Be still with Him a few more moments today before you start moving and striving. Ask for an increase in faith.

Understand that you don't live this one, holy life under your own power. You live it by the grace of God and He will grant you the strength necessary to live it according to His holy will.

Then, make a plan. After Easter, when this book is finished, how will you continue to be open to the good work He has begun in you through this time of Scripture study?

Make a plan.

Don't stop listening to His Word.

ELIZABETH FOSS

BE STILL WITH HIM
A FEW MORE MOMENTS
TODAY BEFORE YOU
START MOVING
AND STRIVING.
ASK FOR AN
INCREASE
IN FAITH.

LECTIO DIVINA

James 2:14-24
James, traditionally considered the first bishop of Jerusalem, writes this letter in his role as a spiritual father to his readers, giving them encouragement and spiritual direction. He is concerned with practical Christian living. In today's passage, James writes that if the readers believe the right things, but fail in living according to those beliefs, their faith is useless. With faith springs a desire to work for the glory of God.

MEDITATIO

What personal message does the text have for me?

ORATIO

What do I say to the Lord in response to His word?

CONTEMPLATIO

What conversion of mind, heart, and life is He asking of me today?

How did I progress in living the Word today?

ACTIO

How will I make my life a gift for others in charity?

What does God want me to do today?

REPENT

When you do good works, are you offering them to God or do you do them because you think you can earn heaven or because they make you feel better about yourself?

Do you spend more time doing good things which make you feel like a good person than you do getting to know the heart of the good God?

RESTORE

What is the plan for remaining in close relationship with the Lord in Scripture after this study ends?

GIVE THANKS

Think of the times recently when you drew close to our Lord. Now consider the times your love for Him overflowed into love for the people in your life.

PRAY

Lord, I hear You say,
"Everything is possible to one who has faith."
And I reply, with all my heart,
"I do believe, help my unbelief!"

MARK 9:23-24

wednesday

DEUTERONOMY 7: 6-9

For you are a people holy to the Lord your God; the Lord your God has chosen you out of all the peoples on earth to be his people, his treasured possession.

It was not because you were more numerous than any other people that the Lord set his heart on you and chose you—for you were the fewest of all peoples. It was because the Lord loved you and kept the oath that he swore to your ancestors, that the Lord has brought you out with a mighty hand, and redeemed you from the house of slavery, from the hand of Pharaoh king of Egypt. Know therefore that the Lord your God is God, the faithful God who maintains covenant loyalty with those who love him and keep his commandments, to a thousand generations...

FOR FURTHER CONTEMPLATION:

ROMANS 15:18

1 CORINTHIANS 15:10

PHILIPPIANS 2:12-8

I wish I could sing the verses from Philippians to you. My children all know this passage in song and it's so very useful when they begin to complain and bicker. Children need frequent reminders to do their best without arguing or complaining.

I find, though, that grown women rarely need to be reminded not to grumble or argue in the face of duties. We know we're not supposed to complain. We know that the weariness that creeps into our voices and snaps at the people closest to us is not beyond reproach. We know that the irritation that we allow to take root as we do the mundane without any acknowledgement or gratitude is dangerously close to becoming an overgrown bramble in our souls.

We know. And we despair because now we've complained about our work and added the sin of complaint to our discontent.

There.

There, in our despair, we've sinned yet again, moving perilously close to a carnival's mirror within a mirror without end until we've fallen into utter contempt for ourselves.

Just stop.

Stop striving for perfection. It is pride (again, I know) that stirs this muddiness in our souls. It is trying to be good enough and strong enough and, well, just enough enough under our own power that brings us to the brink of despair. Let go of that sinister manifestation of pride.

Know that Christ lived and died for you—to perfect you. Let Him do the work He came to do. He is a faithful God who keeps His merciful covenant, even with you. You don't have to do this work alone. God is at work in you. Get out of His way and let Him do it.

Believing that God is at work in you doesn't mean that you aren't proactive and industrious. It means that you work as for the Lord, with hope and energy and courage and joy. You work for God's pleasure and His purpose. It is God who animates our work with the promise of His grace. Saint Paul reminds us of what God has yet to do in our lives and that reminder gives us hope: He will give us grace for each and every moment, sanctifying each and every encounter according to His good purpose for our benefit now and in eternity.

All the messes. All the challenges. All the broken places. All the hurts—both given and received. He has grace enough and He will pour that grace over us each and every day, moment by moment, sufficient for our good.

The living Christ offers to us the power of future grace. That is the power He offers us for the next moment and the next week and the distant future as we work for His glory.

Ask Him. Every minute of every day, ask for His abundant grace. Let it wash over you and allow Christ to help you with the work of your hands. Allow Him to infuse it with Himself, transforming it into something holy, and wholly beautiful.

And then, share His joy.

ELIZABETH FOSS

Know that Christ lived **and died** for you—to perfect you. Let Him **do the work** He came to do. He is a faithful God **who keeps His merciful covenant**, even with you.

LECTIO DIVINA

LECTIO

Deuteronomy 7:6-9

The fifth book of the Bible, Deuteronomy was also written by Moses. Written around the 1400s B.C., the book's name in Greek means "second law". The book recounts the covenant the people had made with God, and also serves as Moses' farewell discourse. Moses entreats the people to remember God's love for them and to be faithful to the covenant they have made with the Lord.

MEDITATIO

What personal message does the text have for me?

ORATIO

What do I say to the Lord in response to His word?

CONTEMPLATIO

What conversion of mind, heart, and life is He asking of me today?

How did I progress in living the Word today?

ACTIO

How will I make my life a gift for others in charity?
What does God want me to do today?

REPENT

Do you grumble and complain about the duties of this life?

Do you let ingratitude or irritation erode your awareness of God's gracious provision?

Do you despair in your sins and beat yourself up for imperfection, forgetting that you are the dearly loved child of God and He has died to save you from your wretchedness?

RESTORE

What household task is your favorite?

What is your favorite way to steward the shelter God has given you?

Do that with a happy heart today.

GIVE THANKS

When were you given the grace to go about your daily round with a light and cheerful heart?

PRAY

Dear Jesus,
help me to relinquish
my tight grip on perfectionism.
Let me let go of striving.
I want so badly to rest in You.

ABOVE ALL | FIFTH WEEK OF LENT

thursday

1 KINGS 8:51-53A

([F]or they are your people and heritage, which you brought out of Egypt, from the midst of the iron-smelter.) Let your eyes be open to the plea of your servant, and to the plea of your people Israel, listening to them whenever they call to you. For you have separated them from among all the peoples of the earth, to be your heritage.

FOR FURTHER CONTEMPLATION:

JAMES 4:7-8, 10

It is the holy contradiction: stoop low and He will raise you on high. This morning, the reading from First Kings reminds us that we are a holy people with a holy inheritance. God has already called us to Himself and He has made us His very own children. If that's the case, why is all of this stuff called "life" so very hard?

Why is that every year I get to Lent and I want to scrub myself clean and start all over again?

God knows.

Saint James told us all those many years ago that God knew that we would sin and we would backslide and that, no matter how much we wanted to always act as a people set apart for holy goodness, we would falter and fail. Every year, we need Lent.

We need to turn and return to Him.

There is no failure in failing, as long as we fail under His care. When we fail, we acknowledge that we cannot live holy and spotless lives of our own volition. When we fail, we know we need a Savior. It's the knowing the need that brings us to the throne of salvation. It's the humility to see our sinful selves and to stoop low and beg mercy that raises us into our inheritance.

God has set you apart, made a place for you. Draw close to Him, close enough to show Him the times where you think you've failed. Now, draw even closer. Have the courage and the humility to let Him show you even more, to show you how He sees that you've fallen short of His intended glory.

Hold out your hands. Let Him cleanse them. Then, let Him grasp them and take you where He intends you to go.

Lent requires a certain grace and grace requires space. Sin crowds our souls and it fills us with cloudy muck until there's no room for the infusion of grace that God intends. As difficult as it is, a thorough examination of our conscience, a pouring out of our sins and a listening for His merciful chastisement, is the best way to begin this season. Refer, again, to the cumulative list in the back of this journal.

You've done the hard work of examining your conscience, day by day. The reward (though it might not seem so at first) is that you have the tools you need for an excellent Confession before Easter. Over the next few days, make notes for that Confession. Don't edit your conscience as it reminds you what to confess. When you have finished listing your weaknesses and your failings, put the pen down. Then, just listen. Listen hard. Has he nudged you to list something else? Be brave! Write it down. Let it all be driven onto your paper. (Note: Keep the paper with you, in your pocket, safe from anyone else's eyes and where you can add to it when you are prompted by the Lord. Take it to Confession with you. And after Confession, burn it.)

ELIZABETH FOSS

HOLD OUT YOUR HANDS. LET HIM CLEANSE THEM. THEN, LET HIM GRASP THEM AND TAKE YOU WHERE HE INTENDS YOU TO GO.

LECTIO DIVINA

1 Kings 8:51-53a
The First and Second Books of Kings relate the history of the kings and kingdoms of Israel and Judah. Written around 561 B.C., both books depict the importance of the Temple, which was built by King Solomon according to the specifications of the covenant his father, King David, made with God (found in the book 1 Chronicles). In this passage, King Solomon prays before the people during the dedication of the Temple in Jerusalem.

MEDITATIO

What personal message
does the text have for me?

ORATIO

What do I say to the Lord in
response to His word?

CONTEMPLATIO

What conversion of mind,
heart, and life is He asking
of me today?

How did I progress in living the Word today?

ACTIO

How will I make my life a gift for others in charity?
What does God want me to do today?

REPENT

Has your pride kept you from Confession?

RESTORE

Go to your computer, find all available confession times, and write one appointment for yourself into your calendar. Keep the date with your soul for reconciliation.

GIVE THANKS

How has God spoken to you this Lent? How has He convicted you or your sins and shown you how to return to Him?

PRAY

Dear Lord,
I know that confessing my sins aloud
and hearing words of forgiveness are great gifts to me.
Please help me get there, God.
Please remove all the obstacles to a good Confession,
all the logistical details that stand in the way.
Most of all God, please help me to
conquer my own pride to lay myself low
before the throne of Your mercy.

friday

ISAIAH 53:10-12

Yet it was the will of the Lord to crush him with pain.
When you make his life an offering for sin,
   he shall see his offspring, and shall prolong his days;
through him the will of the Lord shall prosper.
   Out of his anguish he shall see light;
he shall find satisfaction through his knowledge.
    The righteous one, my servant, shall make many righteous,
    and he shall bear their iniquities.
Therefore I will allot him a portion with the great,
   and he shall divide the spoil with the strong;
because he poured out himself to death,
   and was numbered with the transgressors;
yet he bore the sin of many,
   and made intercession for the transgressors.

FOR FURTHER CONTEMPLATION:

JEREMIAH 23:24

PSALMS 44:20-21

LUKE 16:14-15

LUKE 8:17

1 JOHN 1:8-9

JAMES 5:16,19-20

Now comes the time of reckoning. Our sins can be counted; we can know them and hate them. We can privately ask God's forgiveness for them. But God asks us not to leave it there. He exhorts us on no uncertain terms to speak them aloud to another person. The Church, in her mercy and her obedience to Scripture, provides for us the place and the person.

When we are alone with our sins, trapping them in the chamber of our minds, we are completely in exile. The paradox before us, as we sit by ourselves knowing that we are sinners, is that the very Gospel to which we've given our lives and with which we've convicted ourselves, offers the grace we need. I am a sinner. And so are you. We are desperately in need of a Savior.

We have One.

He invites us to come as we are, sinful and sorrowful, to the throne of mercy, where He will love us.

We squirm. We don't want to utter those words aloud. We worry about what the priest who hears them will think of us. We forget that the man who sits there sits in Christ's place and his purpose is to give voice to God's words of forgiveness. Jesus already knows with perfect clarity exactly how we've sinned. Whether we kneel in a confessional or not, we cannot hide from Him. He already knows. And He's already paid the price for whatever you've noted on the list you hold in sweaty palms.

There is no getting around this: the Gospel calls us to confession. The Gospel calls us to humble ourselves and bring contrite hearts to Him. The Gospel calls us to beg the grace He wants to give us in order to reconcile Himself with us. And the Gospel calls us to be grateful for the battle He has already won on our behalf.

Something extraordinarily beautiful happens when we speak the words aloud and give our sins a channel out of our souls. Even though it's sometimes excruciatingly difficult, the act of speaking purges the guilt and the fear that binds the sin to us. After we've spoken our sins aloud with contrition, the words of absolution, also spoken aloud, are healing balm to the soul. Sins are forgiven; light is flooded into our darkness. Sanctifying grace is restored to our souls and we are strengthened in very real ways.

It's hard to get there, hard to take the time out of our daily routines, hard to squirm under the contrite examination of our consciences, hard to utter those ugly words of failure aloud. But it's worth it. So worth it.

You're worth it.

Start fresh. Let Him take away your sins. He's already won pardon for your offenses.

ELIZABETH FOSS

He invites us to come as we are, sinful and sorrowful, to the throne of mercy, where He will love us.

LECTIO DIVINA

LECTIO

Isaiah 53:10-12

Isaiah offers the most significant prophetic teaching on the Messiah. Today's verses are from the Song of the Suffering Servant—the man who suffers and dies in order to fulfill the plan of God. This passage is seen as a prediction of the redemptive suffering of Christ. It is also part of the first reading of Good Friday's liturgy.

MEDITATIO

What personal message does the text have for me?

ORATIO

What do I say to the Lord in response to His word?

CONTEMPLATIO

What conversion of mind, heart, and life is He asking of me today?

How did I progress in living the Word today?

ACTIO

How will I make my life a gift for others in charity?

What does God want me to do today?

REPENT

It bears asking again: is your pride keeping you from Confession?

RESTORE

How will you treat yourself to celebrate after confession?

GIVE THANKS

Re-write today's verses from Isaiah as a prayer of thanksgiving. "Thank you, Jesus, for suffering for me and for many so that we might be justified. Thank you for bearing my guilt..." You take it from there.

PRAY

Read your journaling notes aloud to the Lord.
Say the words right out loud for God and everybody
(or nobody else) to hear.

ISAIAH 1:16-18

Wash yourselves; make yourselves clean;
  remove the evil of your doings
  from before my eyes;
cease to do evil,
  learn to do good;
seek justice,
  rescue the oppressed,
defend the orphan,
  plead for the widow.
Come now, let us argue it out
  says the Lord:
though your sins are like scarlet,
  they shall be like snow;
though they are red like crimson,
  they shall become like wool.

FOR FURTHER CONTEMPLATION:

---

2 CORINTHIANS 6:1-10

We are made for community. Even those of us who are naturally quiet and fill up in introverted, solitary ways are called to worship and to serve in community. During Lent, we wash ourselves clean through the ministry of Confession to another and then we go forth to share what the Lord is doing in our lives.

Unless of course, in our pride, we turn in on ourselves instead. Pride turns us away from community. Pride tells us we don't need other people. It takes genuine humility to ask for help, to seek counsel, to trust someone with our hearts.

And wherever two or more are gathered, there will be conflict and ruptured relationships.

God knows that, and He tells us to reconcile with one another.

"All this is from God, who reconciled us to himself through Christ, and has given us the ministry of reconciliation." (2 Corinthians 5:18)

To reconcile is to bring into agreement and harmony, make compatible and consistent. To live a ministry of reconciliation is to live a seamless life, pulling everything together for the glory of God. Nothing is more challenging, more intricate, and more beautiful than when that seamless work calls us to weave the faith into the lives of our neighbors. Sometimes, we share with bold strokes of a pen and frame it for the world to see. More often, we share in quiet moments with one or two hearts. Always, we share with the actions of our ordinary days.

More often, we share in quiet moments with one or two hearts.

Saint Paul reminds the Corinthians to behave in such a way that they cause no one to stumble. I recall that as Saint Paul traveled and spread the Gospel, people thought he was crazy. One Roman governor even said to him, "Paul, you are mad; your great learning is turning you mad." (Acts 26:24 NRSV) Seeming to be crazy in a world lost to sin is not necessarily a bad thing.

Living a life of reconciliation according to the Gospel can look rather crazy in today's climate. We live an upside down life. We replace the pleasures of the world with the true joys of beatitudes. We substitute vice for virtue, often feeling a temporal sting in the doing. Our moments and our hours are dedicated to the ongoing effort to cease doing evil and to learn to do good.

The great learning of Saint Paul's life was his holy understanding of exactly how to live in complete friendship with Christ. And that looked crazy to his neighbors.

What does your crazy look like? How is your life in Christ a stark contrast to the world around you? How does being "mad" challenge you in your walk with your neighbor? What can God give you to help you walk with confidence?

Dear friends in Christ, come now, let us set things right!

Let us reconcile.

Then, we can live the God-honoring life Saint Paul describes. We can embrace the crazy that is God's will for us and we can live out of step with the world, but completely in step with our Savior.

ELIZABETH FOSS

LECTIO DIVINA

Isaiah 1:16-18

During Isaiah's ministry, the Kingdom of Judah was experiencing a period of peace and prosperity, which, while economically beneficial, led to a decline of the people's moral life and brought forth idolatry, corruption, and oppression. In these verses, Isaiah relates God's plea for the people to cleanse themselves of sin and return to their former, more righteous way of living.

MEDITATIO

What personal message does the text have for me?

ORATIO

What do I say to the Lord in response to His word?

CONTEMPLATIO

What conversion of mind, heart, and life is He asking of me today?

How did I progress in living the Word today?

ACTIO

How will I make my life a gift for others in charity?
What does God want me to do today?

REPENT

Do you fail to speak up in the presence of injustice?

Do you fail to share and live your faith boldly, shy about living the seamless life of a committed Christian for all the world to see, no matter where you are?

RESTORE

Sketch a preliminary plan for community.

Can you reach out in hospitality to someone whose friendship you might enjoy and invite someone into your space?

What does that look like?

GIVE THANKS

For the times that you have felt crazy for Christ and that very feeling gave you peace, praise God.

For the people God has given you to walk with on your Christian journey, give genuine and heartfelt thanks. (Maybe even tell them as well as telling God.)

PRAY

Dear Lord,
I know that I am made for community.
I also know that often I feel very much alone.
I'm asking You for two distinct things today.
Please embolden me to speak truth in
my sphere of influence, to bring your peace to
my little corner of the universe.
Please also bless me with companions on the journey,
with like-hearted travelers who can understand
my crazy and help me to be
a better minister of reconciliation.

ABOVE ALL | FIFTH WEEK OF LENT

holy week

EVERY DAY THIS WEEK:

SCRIPTURE READINGS

ESSAY REFLECTION

LECTIO DIVINA

REPENT, RESTORE, GIVE THANKS

PRAYER

MORE THIS WEEK:

WEEKLY SCRIPTURE MEMORY

WEEKLY SCRIPTURE MEMORY

HOLY WEEK

Here, we continue to memorize Colossians 3:12-17.

Over the course of Lent, we will commit to memory the entire passage Paul gives to the Colossians in order to tell them how to live a new life in the Lord. Taking it just a little bit at a time and building week after week, we can commit the passage to memory and—even better—we can hide it in our hearts.

COLOSSIANS 3:17

AND WHATEVER YOU DO, IN WORD OR DEED, DO EVERYTHING IN THE NAME OF THE LORD JESUS, GIVING THANKS TO GOD THE FATHER THROUGH HIM.

do EVERYTHING in the name of the LORD JESUS

COLOSSIANS 3:17

WEEKLY PLANS

SUNDAY

MONDAY

TUESDAY

WEDNESDAY

THURSDAY

FRIDAY

SATURDAY

PRAY + FAST + GIVE

palm sunday

HEBREWS 10:9-18

Then he added, "See, I have come to do your will."

He abolishes the first in order to establish the second. And it is by God's will that we have been sanctified through the offering of the body of Jesus Christ once for all.

And every priest stands day after day at his service, offering again and again the same sacrifices that can never take away sins. But when Christ had offered for all time a single sacrifice for sins, "he sat down at the right hand of God," and since then has been waiting "until his enemies would be made a footstool for his feet." For by a single offering he has perfected for all time those who are sanctified. And the Holy Spirit also testifies to us, for after saying,

"This is the covenant that I will make with them
    after those days, says the Lord:
I will put my laws in their hearts,
    and I will write them on their minds,"

he also adds,

"I will remember their sins and their lawless deeds no more."
Where there is forgiveness of these, there is no longer any offering for sin.

FOR FURTHER CONTEMPLATION:

MARK 11:1-10

JOHN 12:12-16

HOLY WEEK

Today, the Church celebrates Christ's triumphant ride through Jerusalem. To every mother's consternation, the Gospel is exceedingly long on the same day her children are armed with palm leaves that look deceptively benign, but actually make for very sharp swords.

And in my head echoes the children's song: *Here comes Jesus riding on a donkey. Hosanna! Hosanna! Hosanna to the King!*

I am transported back to a time when my biggest worry was keeping Patrick from poking Christian's eye out right there in the third pew from the front, all the way to the left. Back then, I thought that if I just followed all the rules and raised them up right, it would all turn out storybook perfect. Guaranteed.

God has spent the last four years showing me how erroneous and even dangerous that thinking can be.

No matter how many books we read or how earnestly we attempt to do all the right things, we have no guarantee of the way things will turn out. Not upon graduation. Not in our jobs. Not in our marriages. And certainly not in parenting. We just don't know.

Bad things will happen. We live in a fallen world among broken people. You might even reach a period in your life where you begin to peer around every corner because you've learned it's likely a bad thing waits there.

And it might actually be waiting there.

I am struck by the sharp contrast of the jubilant crowd cheering the humble king on the donkey, followed by the battered, naked, broken man hanging, arms outstretched, on an instrument of torture. There it was, the bad thing waiting after the good day.

It seems like such a fairy tale one day, only to be followed by such gripping grief the next.

In those dark seasons of grief, we cling to hope and the assurance of the only guarantee, the only thing that stands even in the bitterest winds of terrible times:

When we share in the cross, we will be made perfect. Our sins will be forgiven, our consciences will be made pure, and we will be fully with God.

He has made a covenant with us. In His time, He will completely heal the ones He sanctifies. When we are baptized in Christ, He does the work of our salvation, perfecting us with His sacrifice. We approach the throne of mercy. It is a sign of contradiction. He sits there a king and a sacrificial offering. He forgives us all our sins and says no further offering is necessary. The king on the cross is the source of our sanctity.

With perfect obedience, Jesus came to do the will of the Father: to save us from our sin and open unto us eternal life with Him. By the grace of God, we know how this—and only this—turns out: we share in the Kingdom of Heaven with a good and glorious God.

ELIZABETH FOSS

By the grace of God, we know how this— and only this—turns out: **we share in the Kingdom of Heaven with a good and glorious God.**

LECTIO DIVINA

Hebrews 10:9-18
One of the significant themes of Hebrews is the superiority of the New Covenant, instituted by Christ, over the Old Covenant found in the Old Testament. This is clearly seen in today's verses, which show how the sacrifice of Jesus on the cross is infinitely superior because it is the sacrifice of Himself, in the Heavenly sanctuary.

MEDITATIO

What personal message
does the text have for me?

ORATIO

What do I say to the Lord in
response to His word?

CONTEMPLATIO

What conversion of mind,
heart, and life is He asking
of me today?

How did I progress in living the Word today?

ACTIO

How will I make my life a gift for others in charity?

What does God want me to do today?

REPENT

Can you trust God with the ending, even as you walk through the very hard moments of the story of your life here on earth, or do you set up unreasonable expectations for earthly outcomes based on your own economy?

RESTORE

Give your mind and your hands permission to dream here.

Just let yourself sketch in some dreams, unchecked by your fear.

What do your fondest hopes look like?

GIVE THANKS

Take a good look back at the hard times in your life so far. Do you see God's work there?

PRAY

I sit still and silent, Lord,
so grateful for Your sacrifice,
so humbled by Your gift,
so willing to grow in holiness.

ABOVE ALL | FIRST WEEK OF LENT

monday

LUKE 22:24-27

A dispute also arose among them as to
which one of them was to be regarded as the
greatest. But he said to them, "The kings of
the Gentiles lord it over them; and those in
authority over them are called benefactors.
But not so with you; rather the greatest
among you must become like the youngest,
and the leader like one who serves. For who is
greater, the one who is at the table or the one
who serves? Is it not the one at the table? But I
am among you as one who serves."

FOR FURTHER CONTEMPLATION:

JEREMIAH 1:5-8

1 PETER 4:10-11

JEREMIAH 29:11-14

It's so easy for me to imagine that scene where the apostles ask who will be the greatest. I have five boys; even with seats assigned since they were very little, the jostling for the Alpha position is well-known around our table.

But we all do it, not just those men who make their competitiveness obvious. We all want the blue ribbon that says we're best. What God wants is for us to forget about our status relative to anyone else and to become the best version of ourselves.

God has a plan for each one of us, a specific calling on our lives. He has given us exactly what we need to carry out His mission for us. Our pride compels us to look around, to superficially judge someone else's mission, to size up her gifts, and moan at our lack. Or, sometimes, our pride pats us on the backs and tells us how much better we are than someone else.

God has a plan for each one of us, a specific calling on our lives.

He has given us exactly what we need to carry out His mission for us.

It's fairly easy to see how when we start looking down on people we're in trouble. C. S. Lewis warns, "A proud man is always looking down on things and people; and, of course, as long as you are looking down, you cannot see something that is above you." (*Mere Christianity*) So focused on self, we cannot see God.

But we're in trouble when we find ourselves inferior to someone else, too. It can seem like when God was giving gifts of grace (talent, beauty, creativity), we got slighted. Instead of seeing that all gifts are God's extravagant blessings on us, and that someone else's gifts can grant us grace, we are so focused on ourselves and our perceived lack that pride whispers despair into those comparisons. We become obsessed to the point of distraction with the idea that someone else is more gifted than we are, or that her gifts get more recognition, or maybe we just really wish we had an entirely different set of gifts—impressive, praise-worthy, noticeable gifts.

God distributes unearned gifts in unequal measure, which means we who compare either spend our time feeling puffed up and superior or downcast and inferior. The truth is that each of us has received a gift and we were given that gift to employ for one another. Those gifts are not accidents. They are entrusted to each of us to give to the Kingdom. If it all feels out of balance, we need to ask ourselves if we're doing what He intended with the gifts chosen for us. One thing is certain: your gifts were not given so that you can gain the admiration of other women. They were given to you so that you can serve. God knows exactly what we need to be able live the life He intended when He created us. When we steward our gifts for His glory—even when that means we suffer for the work—we'll know true contentment with our true lives.

ELIZABETH FOSS

LECTIO DIVINA

LECTIO

Luke 22:24-27
After the institution of the Eucharist at the Last Supper, the disciples are arguing over who is the greatest among them. Jesus tells them that the greatest is the one who serves the others, as He has served them during His lifetime.

MEDITATIO

What personal message does the text have for me?

ORATIO

What do I say to the Lord in response to His word?

CONTEMPLATIO

What conversion of mind, heart, and life is He asking of me today?

How did I progress in living the Word today?

ACTIO

How will I make my life a gift for others in charity?
What does God want me to do today?

REPENT

Do you dishonor God by devaluing the gifts He's given to you? Do you resent others for the gifts they have that you don't?

Do miss your own gifts because you are so focused on other people's gifts?

Do you seek acclamation and affirmation for your gifts, forgetting that they were freely given and not at all earned?

RESTORE

Give a gift today.

Thoughtfully choose one small gift for someone you love.

Take care and time, then experience the joy of a giving an unexpected gift.

GIVE THANKS

You have gifts, specially chosen and graciously given to you. What are they?

List them here and thank Him sincerely.

PRAY

Lord,
I see You and know You
as my maker.
Thank You sincerely for all the gifts
You've given to me.
Increase in me a sense of
gratitude for them
and help me to use
them for
Your glory.

tuesday

1 JOHN 1:5-10

This is the message we have heard from
him and proclaim to you, that God is light
and in him is no darkness at all. If we say we
have fellowship with him while we walk in
darkness, we lie and do not do what is true;
but if we walk in the light as he is himself
in the light, we have fellowship with one
another, and the blood of Jesus his Son
cleanses us from all sin. If we say we have
no sin, we deceive ourselves, and the truth
is not in us. If we confess our sins, he who
is faithful and just will forgive our sins and
cleanse us from all unrighteousness. If we say
that we have not sinned, we make him a liar,
and his word is not in us.

FOR FURTHER CONTEMPLATION:

---

2 CORINTHIANS 4:3-4

HOLY WEEK

We have spent hours this Lent considering pride. When we talk about deadly sins, pride is the deadliest. Pride gives birth to other sins. It's also the most cunning. Pride can take on different shapes so that just when you think you've conquered it, it pops up looking like something altogether different. It is pride to think that we have truly succeeded on our own. God is the source of all our true successes. It is pride when we trumpet those successes so that other people will ooh and ahh at them and give us glory (or fame or followers or likes or page views). Those incidences of pride in our lives are pretty obvious.

It is also pride, though, when we degrade ourselves, when we dwell on our failures and beat ourselves up for our imperfections. Even though we don't look all puffed up, we're still obsessing with ourselves. Pride isn't limited to braggadocio and swagger. Pride can be self-flagellation, too. Either way, we make everything all about ourselves.

About this whole cycle of pride, remember that true humility is not thinking less of ourselves, but thinking of ourselves less. God doesn't want us to be puffed up, nor does He want us to sin against our dignity by pummeling ourselves with His word and beating ourselves up for being imperfect.

A little prayerful introspection is a beautiful thing that can yield countless benefits to our lives. Introspective obsession is the stuff of which rotting souls are made. Look up! Look out!

true humility is not thinking less of ourselves, but thinking of ourselves less

Be genuinely interested in everything but yourself. Be amazed by what God has given to you in nature. The sun comes up every day and lights and warms the world for you, and then you see His glory all around. Morning grass crunches under your feet. Alternatively, there's no frost where you live, but your skies are almost always blue and the air is nearly always warm, with a little bit of an ocean breeze.

Notice. Today, as you go about the ordinary things of your ordinary life, notice how extraordinary the gifts of our Creator are.

And the people? The people who walk with you—the broken, sinful people—are people in His image who bear gifts that will bless you. Look for them!

Pray for the capacity to be amazed by God.

Stop wasting precious time and emotional energy dwelling on yourself. Stop caring so much about the labels and lauds of this world. You are loved by the God of the universe—you, uniquely and distinctly— are cherished by the Almighty.

Confess your sins and be done with them. Step confidently into the light. You are a beloved child of God. Act like it.

ELIZABETH FOSS

LECTIO DIVINA

LECTIO

1 John 1:5-10
Another of the catholic epistles (see Thursday of the first week of Lent), First John was written in Ephesus between 90-100 A.D. John writes to correct false teachings that were leading Christians into error. In this passage, John writes that those who love God keep his commandments, and that no one can declare himself free from sin. The only way to overcome sin is to admit and confess them.

MEDITATIO

What personal message
does the text have for me?

ORATIO

What do I say to the Lord in
response to His word?

CONTEMPLATIO

What conversion of mind,
heart, and life is He asking
of me today?

How did I progress in living the Word today?

ACTIO

Be amazed by God. Look around. What amazes you?
Paint or draw or paste pictures here.
Try, however feebly, to capture just a little
of His great glory.

PRAY

Jesus,
pick my chin up off my chest
and make me look up.
Help me to see You and Your infinite wonder.
Help me to see the people You've given into my life.
And please, Lord, make me grateful.

ABOVE ALL | HOLY WEEK

wednesday

MATTHEW 26:14-16, 20-25

Then one of the twelve, who was called Judas
Iscariot, went to the chief priests and said,
"What will you give me if I betray him to you?"
They paid him thirty pieces of silver. And
from that moment he began to look for an
opportunity to betray him...

When it was evening, [Jesus] took his place
with the twelve; and while they were eating,
he said, "Truly I tell you, one of you will betray
me." And they became greatly distressed
and began to say to him one after another,
"Surely not I, Lord?" He answered, "The one
who has dipped his hand into the bowl with
me will betray me. The Son of Man goes as
it is written of him, but woe to that one by
whom the Son of Man is betrayed! It would
have been better for that one not to have been
born." Judas, who betrayed him, said, "Surely
not I, Rabbi?" He replied, "You have said so."

FOR FURTHER CONTEMPLATION:

MATTHEW 27:3-5

How much time have you spent thinking about Judas, really pondering his character? We tend to shudder at his sin, horror that it is, but we also consider it from afar. Judas is a character so horrible he has very little to do with me.

Except he is me.

He is greedy, accepting 30 pieces of silver in exchange for the life of the Lord. He is perhaps power-hungry and envious, feeling eclipsed by the master he was following. He is faint of heart, overburdened by the life that Jesus was calling him to live.

Or maybe he's none of those, in particular.

EXCEPT HE IS ME.

Maybe Judas is me every time I've sized someone up and wondered how knowing them, befriending them, drawing close to them can benefit me. Maybe Judas is everyone who has stepped on a friend in order to get where she wants to go.

It's okay to use your friends. I love it when a friend calls and says she'll be flying in or out of the airport close by and needs a place to spend the night. I love the chance to gather a friend's little girl into our house for a three-day snowstorm while her parents work 24-hour shifts running a plow business. Use me: I'm here for you.

But Judas? Judas was the abusive friend who sees a person as a potential "friend" only in light of how that person can increase his status or expand his network or enlarge his wallet. A shrewd manipulator, Judas had hitched himself to Jesus because he saw the potential there, the rise to power, the kind of Messiah who would bring him to a secure and prosperous future.

As Judas grappled with the material poverty of the disciples' life and "unpopularity" to the point of hiding to protect themselves, he began to understand that this was not a rising star, but a humble, sacrificial victim. Judas wanted to play for the winning team; he wanted to be first. Instead, he found himself in the Upper Room with a suffering servant who insisted that the first shall be last.

So Judas had no more use for Jesus. He sold him out. He put an end to the utilitarian friendship, but not without trying to gain something more for himself before it was over.

Jesus teaches us so much about human relationships through his own friendships. One of his final lessons is the tormented agony of the man who uses people—not abuses people—for personal gain. Ironically, at the end of his life, no one has any use for the man who used the Lord. They can't even be bothered to punish him.

Judas kills himself.

ELIZABETH FOSS

LECTIO DIVINA

LECTIO

Matthew 26:14-16, 20-25
Judas—under the influence of Satan (see Luke 22:3)—agrees to betray Jesus to the chief priests for the price of 30 pieces of silver, the price of a slave.

MEDITATIO

What personal message does the text have for me?

ORATIO

What do I say to the Lord in response to His word?

CONTEMPLATIO

What conversion of mind, heart, and life is He asking of me today?

How did I progress in living the Word today?

ACTIO

How will I make my life a gift for others in charity?
What does God want me to do today?

REPENT

Take a serious look at the people in your life. Which ones are there because you think you can get something from them?

Spend some time honestly considering the warning that Judas' story has for you.

RESTORE

Spend some time today—preferably in person—connecting in a meaningful way with someone who lifts you up.

Relax into that relationship.

GIVE THANKS

Who are the friends you call when you have reached the end of yourself and need someone to genuinely meet your needs with love?

PRAY

Dear Lord,
You show me that people
who make a practice of using others instead
of genuinely investing in real friendships
are people who die alone.
Help me to be aware
of the way that I manipulate people
for my own gain and show me
how to look for genuine opportunities
to love well instead.

ABOVE ALL | HOLY WEEK

holy thursday

JOHN 13:1-16

Now before the festival of the Passover, Jesus knew that his hour had come to depart from this world and go to the Father. Having loved his own who were in the world, he loved them to the end. The devil had already put it into the heart of Judas son of Simon Iscariot to betray him. And during supper Jesus, knowing that the Father had given all things into his hands, and that he had come from God and was going to God, got up from the table, took off his outer robe, and tied a towel around himself. Then he poured water into a basin and began to wash the disciples' feet and to wipe them with the towel that was tied around him. He came to Simon Peter, who said to him, "Lord, are you going to wash my feet?" Jesus answered, "You do not know now what I am doing, but later you will understand." Peter said to him, "You will never wash my feet." Jesus answered, "Unless I wash you, you have no share with me." Simon Peter said to him, "Lord, not my feet only but also my hands and my head!" Jesus said to him, "One who has bathed does not need to wash, except for the feet, but is entirely clean. And you are clean, though not all of you." For he knew who was to betray him; for this reason he said, "Not all of you are clean."

After he had washed their feet, had put on his robe, and had returned to the table, he said to them, "Do you know what I have done to you? You call me Teacher and Lord—and you are right, for that is what I am. So if I, your Lord and Teacher, have washed your feet, you also ought to wash one another's feet. For I have set you an example, that you also should do as I have done to you. Very truly, I tell you, servants are not greater than their master, nor are messengers greater than the one who sent them."

FOR FURTHER CONTEMPLATION:

ROMANS 10:14-15

PSALM 119:105

HOLY WEEK

Sit with me a moment in the Upper Room. Gathered there are Jesus' dearest friends. Gathered, too, are you and I. We are the ones He loved when we were in the world, the ones He loved to the end. We come grubby, grimy, dirty with the dust of the journey through the streets to follow the Lord. The Lord gives us the Eucharist. He offers His entire body for us and yet John's Gospel doesn't tell that story. He tells the story of the ugly feet instead. In the Eucharist, Jesus gives us Himself as a living sacrifice. In the washing of the feet, He shows us how to give ourselves to one another.

The God of the Universe wants to wash the feet of His friends. Peter demurs. He doesn't want the Lord to hold the dirt of his journey in His hands. Like us, Peter thinks he knows what God wants, but he's off the mark. He thinks he's showing respect to Jesus by refusing to let Him wash his feet. He thinks he's being humble before God. We are reminded of all the times we mistake pride for humility and miss the way that God wants to use us and teach us.

IN THE EUCHARIST, JESUS GIVES US HIMSELF AS A *LIVING SACRIFICE*.

IN THE WASHING OF THE FEET, HE SHOWS US **HOW TO *GIVE OURSELVES* TO ONE ANOTHER.**

Jesus doesn't give Peter a choice. He insists. These were not pretty pedicured feet; they were rough, smelly, weathered feet. They were ugly, and He took them in His holy hands and tenderly washed them clean. When He did so, He left for us a beautiful example of how to receive. We learn from Peter and Jesus how to be served by Jesus and then to turn and serve the people to whom He calls us to minister.

The journey is no longer a singular one. From this day on, Peter's feet will walk in Christ's footsteps; they will go to do Christ's work. Jesus shows Peter how. He says do this the way I do this. He tells Peter it's non-negotiable; to have a part in Him, he must allow the Lord to wash His feet. Jesus washes Peter so that Peter truly understands what servant-love is. Peter allows himself to sit, vulnerable, heart open to accepting the ministry of love. Then, as the realization of what he is being offered dawns, Peter begs Jesus to wash his whole self. He's all in. He knows that he, too, will kneel in humility and love selflessly.

In the words attributed to Saint Augustine, "Do you wish to rise? Begin by descending. You plan a tower that will pierce the clouds? Lay first the foundation of humility."

You want to build the Kingdom of God? Kneel and take the dirtiest aching parts of another and tenderly wash them clean.

Blessed are your feet washed by His hands. They go forth to carry you to share the Good News.

ELIZABETH FOSS

LECTIO DIVINA

LECTIO

John 13:1-16
Washing people's feet was a gesture of hospitality normally performed by a household slave, not the host. Jesus humbles himself to serve His disciples, echoing what Jesus said in Monday's reading from Luke—that the greatest is the one who serves. We must pattern our lives after Jesus, whose actions show us how to love and honor God.

MEDITATIO

What personal message
does the text have for me?

ORATIO

What do I say to the Lord in
response to His word?

CONTEMPLATIO

What conversion of mind,
heart, and life is He asking
of me today?

How did I progress in living the Word today?

300

ABOVE ALL | HOLY WEEK

ACTIO

Holy Thursday
REFLECTION

Where will your holy feet take you this Easter
season? How will you share the Gospel there?

PRAY

I am amazed, dear Jesus,
as I see You kneel in front of me,
taking my feet tenderly into Your hands.
Let me never forget this gesture.
Let me kneel every day
with the same tenderness
for someone
in my life.

ABOVE ALL | HOLY WEEK

good friday

COLOSSIANS 3:12-15

As God's chosen ones, holy and beloved,
clothe yourselves with compassion, kindness,
humility, meekness, and patience. Bear with
one another and, if anyone has a complaint
against another, forgive each other; just as
the Lord has forgiven you, so you also must
forgive. Above all, clothe yourselves with love,
which binds everything together in perfect
harmony. And let the peace of Christ rule in
your hearts, to which indeed you were called
in the one body. And be thankful.

Yes. Here we are, praying on Colossians 3 again. Have you memorized it yet?

Today, as a hush falls over the whole world between 12:00 and 3:00, I contemplate the cross. I squint up Calvary's hill at an instrument of torture, where God-made-man, holy and pure, hangs bloodied and broken to free me from sin.

An instrument of torture. He suffered and died there.

I was recently given a lovely gift of a silver and gold crucifix necklace. The cross is made of smooth gold hanging from a gold chain. The corpus is made of silver. It is clean and bright and very beautiful. I wear it as a sign of contradiction.

The horrible reality of the instrument of torture is transformed into the glorious symbol of my redemption as a child of Christ. I lift it gently from a velvet box and clasp it securely around my neck. I put on love.

And there I stand in the shadow of the cross, one of God's chosen ones. With His mother and Saint John the Beloved, I am suffused with compassion. I enter into His suffering, His passion.

Com * Passion = suffering with

I am united with Him in His suffering. I willingly cross the threshold into a life of compassionate love. There will be sorrow; this won't be easy, but He binds me to His body in perfect harmony and His peace rules in my heart.

This is the life to which I've been called.

This is holiness.

I am so thankful.

ELIZABETH FOSS

**HIS
PEACE
RULES
MY
HEART.**

LECTIO DIVINA

LECTIO

Colossians 3:12-15
Love is the crowning virtue of the Christian life. Throughout Lent, we have been working to put on love and leave our former way of life behind. Christ's love for us was so profound that it led to His death. Today, let us put to death the old man, and put on new life in Christ, in imitation of His love for us.

MEDITATIO

What personal message does the text have for me?

ORATIO

What do I say to the Lord in response to His word?

CONTEMPLATIO

What conversion of mind, heart, and life is He asking of me today?

How did I progress in living the Word today?

Good Friday
REFLECTION

Stand for a few moments, at the foot of the
cross, with Saint John the Beloved and Jesus'
sorrowful mother. Enter into the passion. Be
filled with compassion.

PRAY

I sit still and silent, Lord,
so grateful for Your sacrifice,
so humbled by Your gift,
so willing to grow
in holiness.

ABOVE ALL | HOLY WEEK

holy saturday

MATTHEW 27:62-66

The next day, that is, after the day of Preparation, the chief priests and the Pharisees gathered before Pilate and said, "Sir, we remember what that impostor said while he was still alive, 'After three days I will rise again.' Therefore command the tomb to be made secure until the third day; otherwise his disciples may go and steal him away, and tell the people, 'He has been raised from the dead,' and the last deception would be worse than the first." Pilate said to them, "You have a guard of soldiers; go, make it as secure as you can." So they went with the guard and made the tomb secure by sealing the stone.

There is a quiet stillness to this day. It is the only day of the liturgical year when Christ is dead from morning to evening. There is no Mass today; tonight's Easter Vigil Mass belongs to tomorrow's resurrection. Instead, the church is dark and quiet. Even the Eucharist is not offered today, unless there is danger of death. Can you wait in the silence? Can you still yourself and let part of today be quiet, away from the noises of your world? Can you be still and silent enough to take one more good look at your soul?

I wonder about the guard standing sentry over Jesus' tomb. He was charged with the impossible. Even the chief priests and Pharisees who had offered Christ up to death had enough of a niggling doubt that they asked for a guard at the tomb. And that man stood there knowing that if the tomb were somehow to turn up empty, he would certainly be executed in blame.

CAN YOU WAIT IN THE **SILENCE**? CAN YOU STILL YOURSELF AND LET PART OF TODAY BE **QUIET**, AWAY FROM THE NOISES OF YOUR WORLD? CAN YOU **BE STILL** AND SILENT ENOUGH TO **TAKE ONE MORE GOOD LOOK AT YOUR SOUL?**

The Pharisees wanted that tomb locked up tight, with death sealed in. They weren't taking any chances on hope. They were steeling themselves against the possibility that this story ended in anything but total loss. They certainly weren't looking out for a resurrection.

But we are.

We sit in the sad silence of this day knowing how this story ends. We sit in the anticipated grace of tomorrow and the real grace of reconciliation. We sit in friendship with Jesus Christ and together we look one more time at the tomb.

Can you be silent with Him? Can you take a few moments from this very busy pre-holiday day to sit in silence with our Lord and give thanks for the gift of His holy friendship these six weeks? When we are still and quiet, God has a chance to seep into our souls. So often, we are afraid to be still and silent. We are afraid of the illumination of our souls that silence offers. His voice can be heard in the quiet, and He is gently showing us what He sees inside the tombs of our lives.

One day remains before the stone is rolled away, before He rises in glorious triumph over sin. You have a tomb of your own. Even with all the work you've done, chances are something still remains sealed up tight. What lies locked up in your tomb? What still remains, stubbornly resisting the light of day, hiding there in darkness? Is there anyone still to forgive? Is there anything yet to repent? Is there any remnant of fear, of doubt, of loss that stubbornly resists the gospel of the resurrection? Can you let the crucified Lord roll the stone away and release the remnants of life outside His friendship, or are you standing guard over the tomb of your old self?

"Sleeper, awake!
Rise from the dead,
and Christ will shine on you."

EPHESIANS 5:14

ELIZABETH FOSS

LECTIO DIVINA

LECTIO

Matthew 27:62-66
After Jesus' crucifixion and burial in the tomb of Joseph of Arimathea, the priests and Pharisees ask Pilate to place a guard around the tomb, to prevent Jesus' disciples from stealing the body and claiming Jesus had been raised from the dead. It is likely that the guards would have been punished by death when it was discovered that Jesus' body disappeared from the tomb.

MEDITATIO

What personal message does the text have for me?

ORATIO

What do I say to the Lord in response to His word?

CONTEMPLATIO

What conversion of mind, heart, and life is He asking of me today?

How did I progress in living the Word today?

ACTIO

Holy Saturday
REFLECTION

What lies locked up in your tomb? What still remains, stubbornly resisting the light of day, hiding there in darkness? Is there anyone still to forgive? Is there anything yet to repent? Is there any remnant of fear, of doubt, of loss that stubbornly resists the gospel of the resurrection? Can you let the crucified Lord roll the stone away and release the remnants of life outside His friendship, or are you standing guard over the tomb of your old self?

PRAY

Dear Lord,
with Your strength,
I roll away the stone that traps my sins
and I rise to the light of a life
of Christian service.

WHAT
STILL REMAINS,
STUBBORNLY
RESISTING THE
LIGHT OF DAY,
HIDING THERE
IN DARKNESS?
IS THERE
ANYONE
STILL TO
FORGIVE?

WEEKLY SCRIPTURE MEMORY

EASTER SUNDAY

For Easter, we put it all together, summarizing in these key verses the journey we've taken throughout Lent. Rejoice and be glad in the new garment with which He clothes you!

COLOSSIANS 3:12-17

AS GOD'S CHOSEN ONES, HOLY AND BELOVED, CLOTHE YOURSELVES WITH COMPASSION, KINDNESS, HUMILITY, MEEKNESS, AND PATIENCE. BEAR WITH ONE ANOTHER AND, IF ANYONE HAS A COMPLAINT AGAINST ANOTHER, FORGIVE EACH OTHER; JUST AS THE LORD HAS FORGIVEN YOU, SO YOU ALSO MUST FORGIVE. ABOVE ALL, CLOTHE YOURSELVES WITH LOVE, WHICH BINDS EVERYTHING TOGETHER IN PERFECT HARMONY. AND LET THE PEACE OF CHRIST RULE IN YOUR HEARTS, TO WHICH INDEED YOU WERE CALLED IN THE ONE BODY. AND BE THANKFUL. LET THE WORD OF CHRIST DWELL IN YOU RICHLY; TEACH AND ADMONISH ONE ANOTHER IN ALL WISDOM; AND WITH GRATITUDE IN YOUR HEARTS SING PSALMS, HYMNS, AND SPIRITUAL SONGS TO GOD. AND WHATEVER YOU DO, IN WORD OR DEED, DO EVERYTHING IN THE NAME OF THE LORD JESUS, GIVING THANKS TO GOD THE FATHER THROUGH HIM.

YOU ARE

chosen, holy, & beloved.

COLOSSiANS 3:12

A Christian should be an alleluia from head to foot.
(attributed to Saint Augustine)

JOHN 20:1-18

Early on the first day of the week, while it was still dark, Mary Magdalene came to the tomb and saw that the stone had been removed from the tomb. So she ran and went to Simon Peter and the other disciple, the one whom Jesus loved, and said to them, "They have taken the Lord out of the tomb, and we do not know where they have laid him." Then Peter and the other disciple set out and went toward the tomb. The two were running together, but the other disciple outran Peter and reached the tomb first. He bent down to look in and saw the linen wrappings lying there, but he did not go in. Then Simon Peter came, following him, and went into the tomb. He saw the linen wrappings lying there, and the cloth that had been on Jesus' head, not lying with the linen wrappings but rolled up in a place by itself. Then the other disciple, who reached the tomb first, also went in, and he saw and believed; for as yet they did not understand the scripture, that he must rise from the dead. Then the disciples returned to their homes.

But Mary stood weeping outside the tomb. As she wept, she bent over to look into the tomb; and she saw two angels in white, sitting where the body of Jesus had been lying, one at the head and the other at the feet. They said to her, "Woman, why are you weeping?" She said to them, "They have taken away my Lord, and I do not know where they have laid him." When she had said this, she turned around and saw Jesus standing there, but she did not know that it was Jesus. Jesus said to her, "Woman, why are you weeping? Whom are you looking for?" Supposing him to be the gardener, she said to him, "Sir, if you have carried him away, tell me where you have laid him, and I will take him away." Jesus said to her, "Mary!" She turned and said to him in Hebrew, "Rabbouni!" (which means Teacher). Jesus said to her, "Do not hold on to me, because I have not yet ascended to the Father. But go to my brothers and say to them, 'I am ascending to my Father and your Father, to my God and your God.'" Mary Magdalene went and announced to the disciples, "I have seen the Lord"; and she told them that he had said these things to her.

easter sunday

REVELATION 19:1-9

After this I heard what seemed to be the loud voice of a great multitude in heaven, saying,

"Hallelujah!
Salvation and glory and power to our God,
    for his judgments are true and just;
he has judged the great whore
    who corrupted the earth with her fornication,
and he has avenged on her the blood of his servants."
Once more they said,
"Hallelujah!
The smoke goes up from her forever and ever."
And the twenty-four elders and the four living creatures fell down and worshiped God who is seated on the throne, saying,
"Amen. Hallelujah!"
And from the throne came a voice saying,
"Praise our God,
    all you his servants,
and all who fear him,
    small and great."
Then I heard what seemed to be the voice of a great multitude, like the sound of many waters and like the sound of mighty thunderpeals, crying out,
"Hallelujah!
For the Lord our God
    the Almighty reigns.
Let us rejoice and exult
    and give him the glory,
for the marriage of the Lamb has come,
    and his bride has made herself ready;
to her it has been granted to be clothed
    with fine linen, bright and pure"—
for the fine linen is the righteous deeds of the saints.
And the angel said to me, "Write this: Blessed are those who are invited to the marriage supper of the Lamb." And he said to me, "These are true words of God."

I love John's Easter Gospel best (and I'm sure he'd be glad to know that). John is sure to tell us that he is the disciple whom Jesus loved. And he goes on to tell us that in a foot race with Peter, he's the winner. John is all the young men in my life whom I love!

Peter and John rush in and look around and they leave without seeing the risen Christ.

Mary Magdalene approaches quietly. She is weeping, overcome with her grief. And in her sorrow, so consumed by grief, she is blinded to God, alive before her. If you are a woman who has known grief, you can understand how Mary Magdalene mistook Jesus for the gardener. Grief is blinding, numbing, dumbing.

He is gentle with her, sweet and a little mischievous even, as He reveals the wonderful news to His dear friend. And at the sound of Jesus calling her name, she recognizes Him.

Can you hear Him calling you? He's beckoning you into the life of an Easter person. He's promising you the joys of the Resurrection.

He wants you to shout "Hallelujah!" at the mouth of the empty tomb. Then, run! Run with joy to tell all about it!

Hallelujah means "Praise the Lord!" *Hallelu* is the Hebrew second person imperative: you go praise. And *jah* is the short form of the dear name of the personal God of Israel: Yahweh.

Go praise your personal and living God.

Sing it. Shout it! Dance a jig to it with your children.

Pope Saint John Paul II reminded us that we are an Easter people and Alleluia is our song. Be an Easter person from head to foot.

Go forth and glorify God with your life.

ELIZABETH FOSS

EXAMINATON OF CONSCIENCE

Here you will find all the daily examination of conscience questions that you've considered this Lent. They are presented here in one of three possible categories, divided according to three root sins: pride, vanity, and sensuality.

Sins of pride are the ones where we seek meaning in our own perceived "successes." We puff ourselves up and wrest power away from God. The sins clustered under vanity are those rooted in a disordered attachment to the world's affirmation and applause. Sensuality seeks pleasure, ease, and comfort, particularly of the flesh.

Of course excellent achievements and human interaction and pleasure are not sins. Making idols of them is. The meaning in our lives should not come from attachments to anything other than God. These questions, gathered this way, are intended to help you prepare for Confession, so that disordered attachments and the things they compel us to do can be forgiven and we can move forward in grace, with God at the center of our lives.

PRIDE

Do I try to figure out a problem on my own, forgetting to ask God for His direction before even attempting to discern the path forward?

Do I think more of book smarts than I do of knowledge of the nature of God?

Am I puffed up by accolades of this world; do I set my goals according to what lofty award or promotion or grad school admission I want to attain, failing to discern if those are God's goals for me?

Do I worry excessively, and fail to hand over my fears to God?

When I perform good works, am I offering them to God or doing them because I think I can earn heaven?

Do I do good works because they make me feel better about myself?

Do I fail to offer God all the little details of my life and do I stubbornly hold on to some illusion of control?

Do I fail to pray about the little details?

Do I despair in my sins and beat myself up for imperfection, forgetting that I am the dearly loved child of God and He has died to save me from my wretchedness?

Has my pride kept me from Confession?

PRIDE

Do I fall prey to the lie that I don't need friends, don't need companions on a Christian journey?

Do I criticize harshly or without mercy?

Do I dismiss other people as beneath me, not worth my time or attention or friendship, because I think that I am exalted above them?

Am I quick to judge other people and find them lacking?

Do I make quick, critical assessments of others without considering them with empathy?

Do I genuinely believe that I am rarely wrong?

Do I cower and weep or lash out in anger at the suggestion I could be wrong?

Do I withhold apology because I think it weakens me?

Do I miss the cues that I have hurt someone else because I'm too preoccupied with myself?

Do I fail to spend my Sundays genuinely worshipping and resting?

Do I despair, thinking that I will never truly conquer sin, never grow in holiness?

Am I prioritizing my life according to God's will?

Am I confused about which responsibilities are mine and which are God's?

PRIDE

Do I slow down and trust that God will provide everything I need?

In my anger, have I sinned against the dignity of another person?

Do I consider someone worth my time and attention only when he or she meets a certain social or economic criteria?

Do I dishonor God by devaluing the gifts He's given to me?

Do I seek acclamation and affirmation for my gifts, forgetting that they were freely given and not at all earned?

Have I failed to apologize promptly, stubbornly digging into my own self-righteousness and sacrificing genuine reconciliation?

Have I apologized insincerely, shifting the responsibility from my own failings and blaming the hurt on the victim of my sins?

VANITY

Do I spend more time on social media than I do in the word of God?

Do I fail to speak up in the presence of injustice?

Am I shy about living the seamless life of a committed Christian for all the world to see, no matter where I am?

Did I lose my patience because I think what I am doing is more important than the person who interrupts me?

Do I judge myself according to the false standards of this fallen world, striving for status or wealth or fame or outward beauty?

Do I think what the crowd thinks or even what just one person thinks is more important than what God thinks? Do I act like I do?

Am I a people pleaser who tries too hard to make everyone like me to the detriment of my own self-worth?

Do I pretend to be a devout Christian, all the while sinning silently inside my head?

Do I demand attention, always seeking the spotlight?

Do I thrive on drama, so I create it in order to sustain the attention of those around me?

Do I recount my faults to others in order to have them reassure me that I am good?

VANITY

Is defensiveness my first reaction to criticism?

Do I live in a false paradigm of cliques and exclusivity to the detriment of knowing and loving all the people God intends for me?

Do I neglect quiet time with God because I am agreeing to do things that fill me with worldly pleasure or acclamation?

Do I withhold hospitality because I think I have to "entertain" in a perfect household?

Am I living according to the world's economy or God's?

Do I miss my own gifts because I am so focused on comparing them to other people's gifts?

Do I use people for my own gain? (Take a serious look at the people in your life. Which ones are there because you think you can get something from them?)

Do I resent others for the gifts they have that I don't?

Do I make a false witness of my life because I'm not honest and sincere about who I really am?

Do I lie, even just a little?

Have I dug up old offenses and opened old wounds in the heat of an argument?

VANITY

Have I ever apologized for something about which I was not sorry or I had no fault, only because I wanted to gain the false peace that comes with avoiding conflict?

Have I made other people the butt of my jokes?

Have I couched gossip in the words of a "prayer request," thereby exposing someone else to the scrutiny of others?

Have I spoken untruths about someone or spread stories whose truth I do not know?

Have I spoken things which are true, but which damage the reputation of another and are better left unsaid?

Am I a backbiter, speaking ill of one member of my family or community to another?

Have I spoken poorly of my spouse, either to my children or to someone outside my family's circle?

SENSUALITY

Do I fail to give my full attention to people when they are talking to me?

Do I spend more time doing good things which make me feel like a good person than I do getting to know the heart of the good God?

Do I fail to share my faith boldly?

Do I fail to notice the need around me because I am so focused on myself?

Do I miss Mass because I've filled the rest of the week so full that I'm too tired to get out of bed on Sunday morning?

Do I miss Mass because the weekend schedule crowds it out?

Do I worry too much about "wasting" time and so work needlessly on Sundays, forgetting that God is the master of time and He has commanded me to rest?

Do I grumble and complain about the duties of this life and lose sight of the blessing of work?

Do I spend too much time in front of screens?

Honestly, how much time do I spend mindlessly clicking around, in search of something to fill my cravings, missing that what I really crave is God?

Do I spend too much time at my job because I don't want to face the work of personal relationships?

Do I favor one of my children (or siblings or parents) over another with my time and attention because it's just easier?

VANITY

Do I fail to give God quality time: still, focused attention every day?

Do I fail to listen carefully to the promptings of the Holy Spirit and/or fail to ask Him to show me how to sanctify my daily round?

Do I let ingratitude or irritation erode my awareness of God's gracious provision?

Am I attached to things of this world and do I make idols of them, prioritizing my life so that I don't have to be without them?

Do I recognize my complete need for Christ and the way that I can be content in Him, or do I focus on the creature comforts in my surroundings?

Have I complained about one child to another?

In my anger, have I lost my temper?

Do I miss the point that all that I have belongs to God for the purpose of extending His love, and so I am miserly with my possessions?

Do I hold back in meeting a need because I'm afraid I won't have enough left for me?

Do I hesitate to invite someone in when I could provide food or shelter or comfort or companionship because it requires work and some bother?

Do I have a right spirit about fasting? Do I wear sackcloth and ashes and moan and complain, or do I embrace sacrifice as a way to become more Christlike?

WE CAN MOVE FORWARD IN GRACE, WITH GOD
AT THE CENTER OF OUR LIVES.

MEET THE AUTHORS

CARLY BUCKHOLZ studied poetry at the University of Virginia before earning a Master's in Higher Education. After five years in Charlottesville, she has moved across the Atlantic for a teaching fellowship in southern England. There, she will teach literature and work in student affairs for the next year. Often next to a pile of books, Carly spends most of her time trying to convince her friends to read more poetry and baking scones. She enjoys writing about her family, her faith, and the Blue Ridge Mountains.

MICAELA DARR lives in Southern California and is a happy wife to her husband, and mother to six charming kiddos (with another bun in the oven). In her former life, she was an elementary and middle school teacher outside the home. Now, as a homeschooling mom, she does both those jobs (and many more) for far less money, but also more joy. She renewed her love of writing by starting a blog when her family took a two year adventure to South Korea, and has since contributed her writing to several other Catholic websites, and two books set to be published in 2018. Her latest out-of-the-home adventure is planning a small Catholic women's conference that aims to strengthen women on their journey to be closer to the God who loves them.

EMILY DEARDO is a lifelong Ohioan and the oldest of three children. Books--writing them, reading them, editing them, talking about them--are her love language. Her first book, Catholic 101, was released in November 2017. When she's not reading, writing, or editing, Emily can be found re-reading Jane Austen, knitting, trying out new recipes, cheering for the Pittsburgh Penguins, or solving the world's problems over a meal with friends. Her writing has been featured on foreverymom.com, and she's twice been a guest on Jennifer Fulwiler's Sirius XM radio show. Emily is currently working on a memoir about life and faith after a double lung transplant. For more, visit her at www.emilymdeardo.com.

ELIZABETH FOSS is a wife, mother, and grandmother. She's happy curled up with a good book or tinkering with a turn of phrase. Long walks make her heart sing and occasionally cause her to break into a run. Though she travels frequently, it's usually only to her beloved Charlottesville, her grandchildren in Connecticut, or the weekend's dictated soccer or dance destination.

MEET THE AUTHORS

ANA HAHN is a wife of nine years and mother of five children. She enjoys educating her three school-aged daughters at home and playing planes with her two toddler boys. In her rare spare time she works on making her home bright and cheerful and sharing bits of that, as well as other motherhood musings, on her blog, Time Flies When You're Having Babies.

MARY LENABURG is a writer, speaker, wife, and mother sharing her witness and testimony about God's redeeming love. Mary has served her local parish in many roles. Now she travels the country and speaks to groups of all ages about God's redeeming love and that faith is the courage to want what God wants for us, even if we cannot see where the path leads. Mary lives in Northern Virginia with her husband of 29 years and her grown son. She continues to embrace her father's advice: "Never quit, never give up, never lose your faith. It's the one reason you walk this earth. For God chose this time and place just for you, so make the most of it."

ALLISON MCGINLEY lives with her husband and two kids in Northern Virginia. When she's not dancing with her daughter or learning about Legos from her son, she writes, sings with a local worship band, and takes pictures of beautiful things. She shares her inspirational photography prints in her Etsy shop, "Be Not Afraid Prints."

LAUREL MUFF is a California girl who loves to travel, write, knit, read, and sing (but not necessarily in that order). She is married to her best friend and they have two beautiful girls together, whom she teaches at home. She loves to gather people around the table for delicious food and great conversation. With a heart for ministry, she is glad to share her faith in whatever capacity the Lord beckons her. She shares her musings on her blog: muffindome.com.

MEET THE AUTHORS

HEATHER RENSHAW is a wife and mother of five living in the missionary territory of the Pacific Northwest. She rarely turns down an opportunity for deep conversation, loud singing, good eating, or silent Adoration. Heather is the author of an eight-week study on the Beatitudes, contributing author of All Things Girl: Truth For Teens, and is currently writing her first book for Catholic mothers. When she's not tackling the myriad tasks of her domestic church, Heather enjoys speaking at events and connecting via Twitter and Instagram (@ RealCatholicMom). Heather may be found at www.RealCatholicMom. com.

KATHRYN WHITAKER, a native Texan, is a wife and mom to six kids, teen to toddler. She shares her perspective on marriage, motherhood, college football, Texas BBQ, and her Catholic faith with honesty and authenticity on her blog, www.teamwhitaker.org. She's a frequent guest on Sirius XM's "The Jennifer Fulwiler Show" but all her kids really care about is what time dinner's ready. In her spare time, she operates her own graphic design business, working primarily with Catholic campus ministry programs around the country.

KATE WICKER is a Catholic wife, mom of five, recovering perfectionist, speaker, and the author of Getting Past Perfect: How to Find Joy & Grace in the Messiness of Motherhood and Weightless: Making Peace with Your Body. Kate is also a senior writer for Catholic Digest and serves as a monthly guest on Relevant Radio's Morning Air Show and Spirit in the Morning. She also has an "almost finished" novel in the works that's been "almost finished" since her she was pregnant with her third baby nearly a decade ago. To learn more about her work and life, visit KateWicker.com.

MEET THE ARTISTS

KRISTIN FOSS is the Art Director and Designer. She is a self-taught watercolor artist who focuses on bright hues and details. With a paintbrush in her hand and fresh blooms in a vase, she finds peace in God's word while putting brush to paper. She lives in New England with her four children and husband. She enjoys creative cooking, thrift stores, nature walks, water, and cotton. You can find her at joyfulmornings.com.

RAKHI MCCORMICK is a Catholic convert from Hinduism and a self-taught, aspiring artist specializing in lettering and whimsical illustrations. Her desire is to spread light into dark places with her art and photography, which can be found in her Etsy shop, Rakstar Designs. Rakhi is happiest alongside her family with a coffee in one hand and a pencil in the other (though fresh floral bouquets are lovely too!). She lives in the Metro Detroit area with her husband and three children and on Instagram at @rakstardesigns.

CHRISTIE PETERS painted the cover and gave us all our mountain motifs. She is an art teacher, illustrator, and co-founder of Every Sacred Sunday, the first NAB Mass journal. Her favorite things include her family, traveling, all things citrus, her little dog Shelby, and the unshakeable beauty of the Catholic Church. Christie is inspired by ordinary people leading extraordinary lives while serving as the hands and feet of Jesus Christ. You can find her at www.christievaughn.com and on Instagram: @christie_vaughn.

BIBLIOGRAPHY

The Bible. She Reads Truth Christian Standard Bible. Holman Bible Publishers, 2017.

The Didache Bible: With Commentaries Based on the Catechism of the Catholic Church. Ignatius Press, 2015.

The Navarre Bible: New Testament Expanded Edition. Four Courts, 2008.

Catechism of the Catholic Church. Second ed. Doubleday, 2003.

Benedict XVI. Post-Synodal Apostolic Exhortation on the Word of God in the Life and Mission of the Church: Verbum Domini. Vatican City, 30 September 2010.

http://w2.vatican.va/content/benedict-xvi/en/apost_exhortations/documents/hf_ben-xvi_exh_20100930_verbum-domini.html. Accessed December 22, 2017.

Hahn, Scott, general editor. *Catholic Bible Dictionary*. Doubleday Religion, 2009.

Hahn, Scott, editor, and Curtis Mitch, compiler. *Ignatius Catholic Study Bible: New Testament*. Ignatius Press, 2010.

Kreeft, Peter. *Back to Virtue*. Ignatius Press, 1992.

---. *Catholic Christianity*. Ignatius Press, 2001.

Neuhaus, John Richard. *Freedom for Ministry*. Revised edition. William B. Eerdmans Publishing Company, 1992.

COLOPHON

This book was printed by CreateSpace, on 55# paper with an interior black and white.
Typefaces used include Museo Slab and Serenity.
The cover is printed in full color with a soft touch matte, full laminate.
Finished size is 7" x 10".

Made in the USA
Middletown, DE
13 February 2018